A-Z IPSW

G000297890

CONTENT

Key to Map Pages	2-3
Large Scale City Centre	4-5
Map Pages	6-65

Index to Streets, Towns, Villages, Hospitals and Selected Places of Interest — 66-84

REFERENCE

A Road	A14
B Road	B1067
Dual Carriageway	
One-way Street	⇒
Traffic flow on A Roads is also indicated by a heavy line on the driver's left.	⇒
Junction Names	COPDOCK MILL INTERCHANGE
Restricted Access	
Pedestrianized Road	
Track & Footpath	===== -----
Residential Walkway	....
Railway	Level Crossing / Station ☰
Built-up Area	NENE DR.
Local Authority Boundary	— ∙ — ∙ —
Posttown Boundary	————
Postcode Boundary within Posttown	— — — —
Map Continuation	30 / Large Scale City Centre 4

Car Park (Selected)	🅿
Church or Chapel	†
Cycleway (Selected)	🚲
Fire Station	■
Hospital	Ⓗ
House Numbers A & B Roads only	37 44
Information Centre	🄸
National Grid Reference	²45
Park & Ride	Ipswich P+🚌
Police Station	▲
Post Office	★
Toilet without facilities for the Disabled	▽
with facilities for the Disabled	▽
Educational Establishment	▢
Hospital or Hospice	▢
Industrial Building	▢
Leisure or Recreational Facility	▢
Place of Interest	▢
Public Building	▢
Shopping Centre or Market	▢
Other Selected Buildings	▢

SCALE

Map Pages 4-5 1:7,920	Map Pages 6-65 1:15,840
8 inches (20.32cm) to 1 mile 12.63 cm to 1 km	4 inches (10.16 cm) to 1 mile 6.31 cm to 1 km

0 ⅛ ¼ Mile
0 100 200 300 400 Metres

0 ¼ ½ Mile
0 250 500 750 Metres

Copyright of Geographers' A-Z Map Company Limited

Head Office :
Fairfield Road, Borough Green, Sevenoaks, Kent TN15 8PP
Telephone: 01732 781000 (Enquiries & Trade Sales)
01732 783422 (Retail Sales)
www.a-zmaps.co.uk
Copyright © Geographers' A-Z Map Co. Ltd.

Ordnance Survey® This product includes mapping data licensed from Ordnance Survey with the permission of the Controller of Her Majesty's Stationery Office.

© Crown Copyright 2004. All rights reserved . Licence number 100017302

EDITION 3 2005

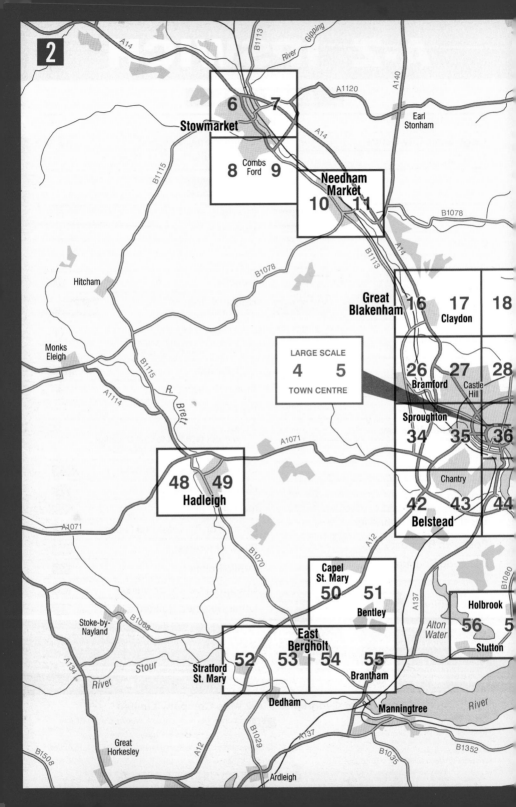

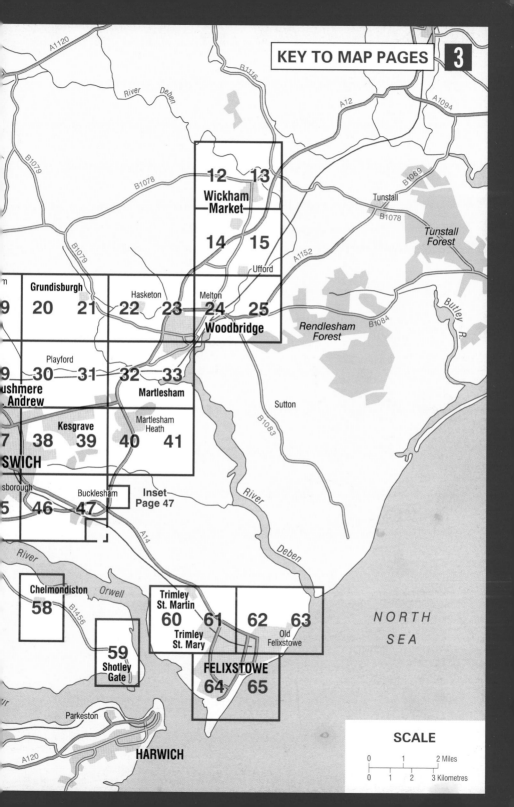

A1120

River Deben

B1116

A12

A1094

B1079

B1078

B1069

Tunstall

B1078

Tunstall Forest

12 13

Wickham Market

14 15

Ufford

A1152

B1084

Butley R.

B1079

Grundisburgh

Hasketon

Melton

Rendlesham Forest

m

9 20 21 22 23 24 25

Woodbridge

Playford

Sutton

9 30 31 32 33

ushmere St. Andrew

Martlesham

B1083

7 38 39 40 41

Kesgrave

Martlesham Heath

SWICH

sborough

Bucklesham

Inset Page 47

River

Deben

5 46 47

A14

River Orwell

B1456

Chelmondiston

58

Trimley St. Martin

60 61 62 63

Trimley St. Mary

Old Felixstowe

NORTH

SEA

59

Shotley Gate

FELIXSTOWE

64 65

Parkeston

A120

HARWICH

SCALE

0   1   2 Miles

0   1   2   3 Kilometres

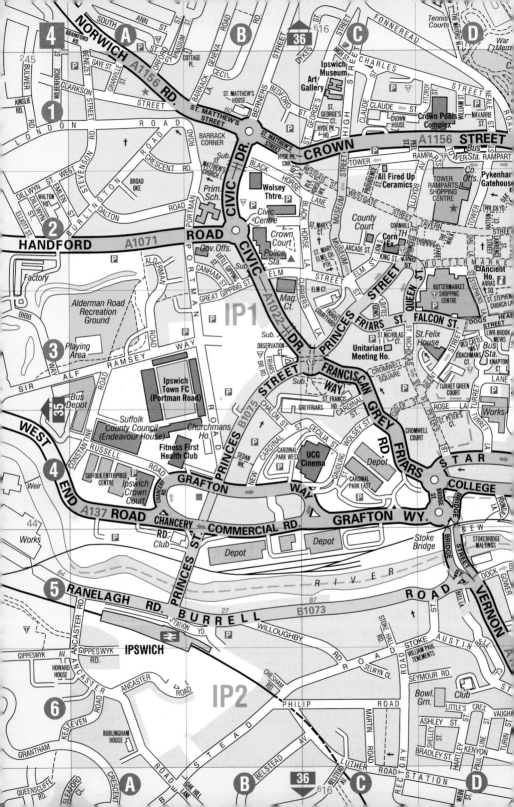

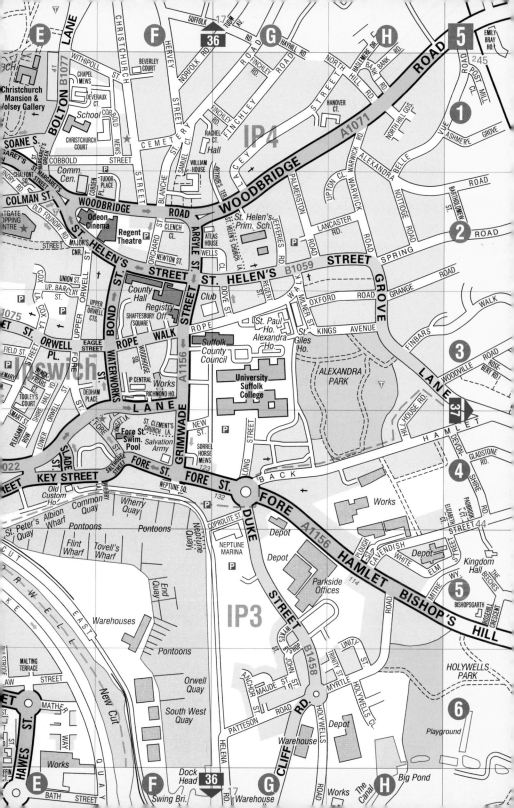

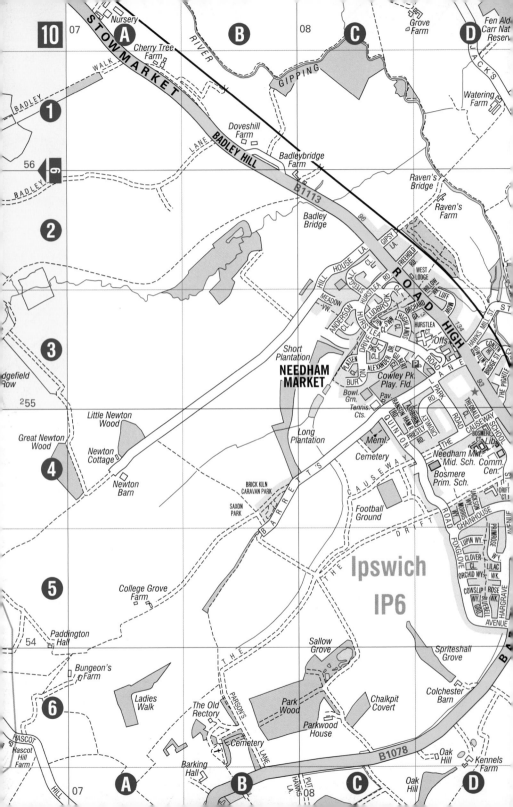

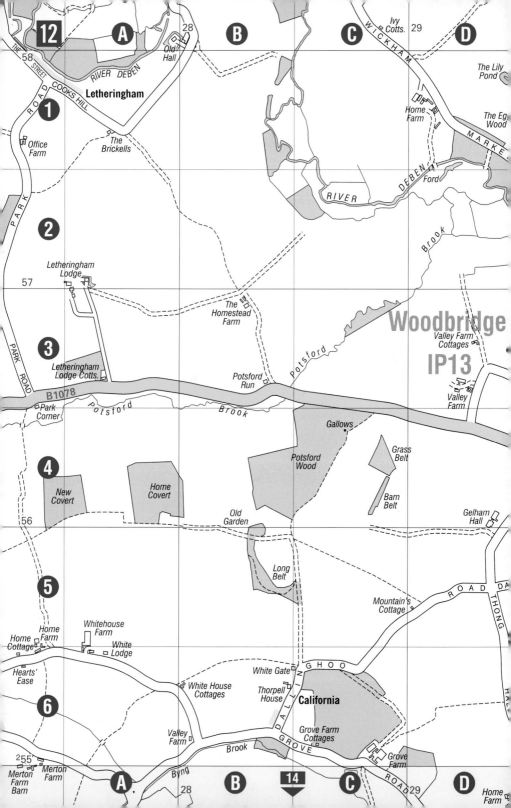

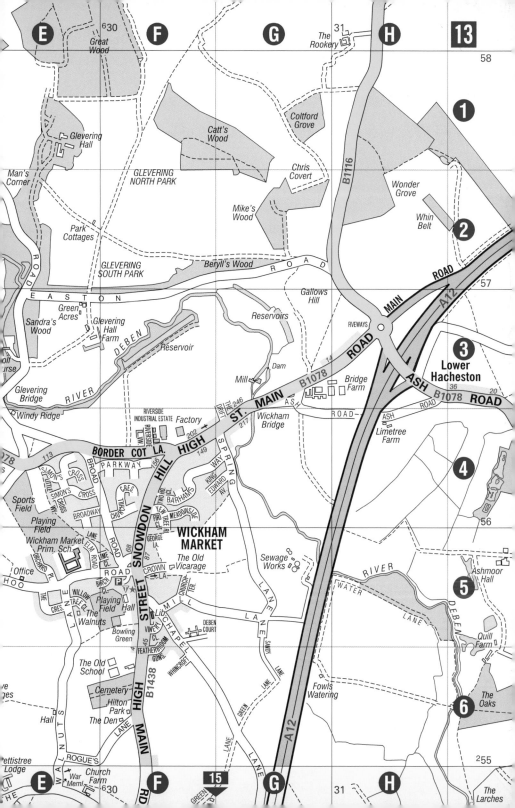

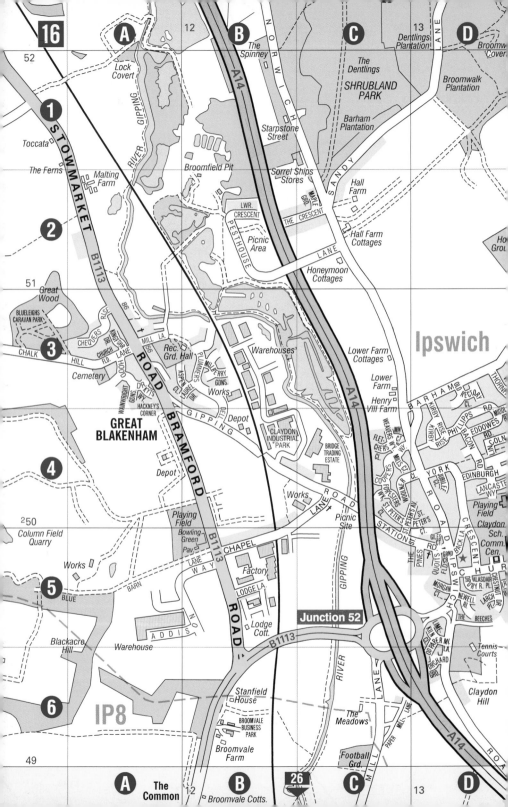

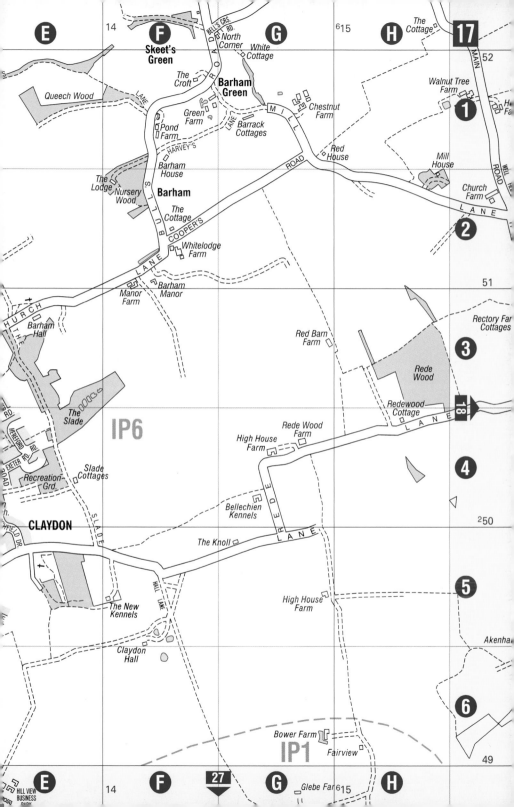

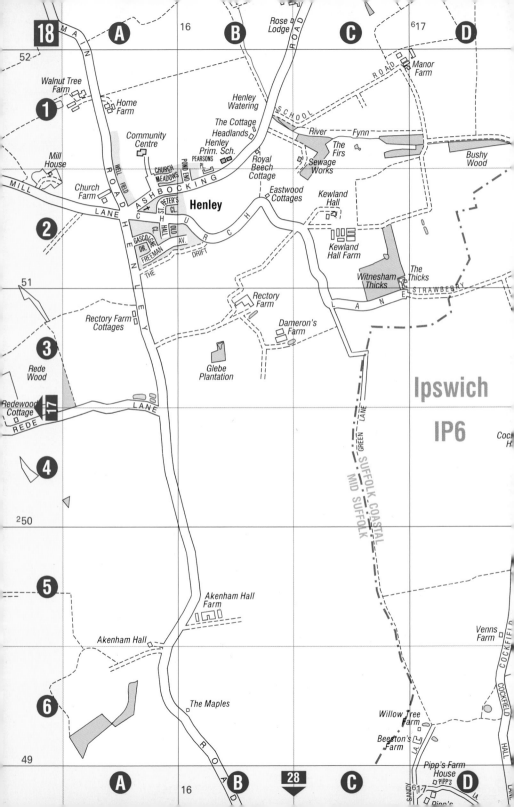

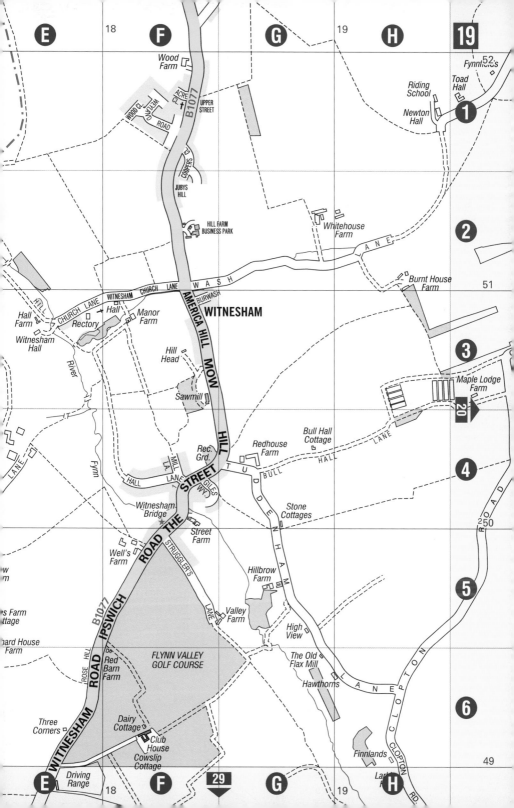

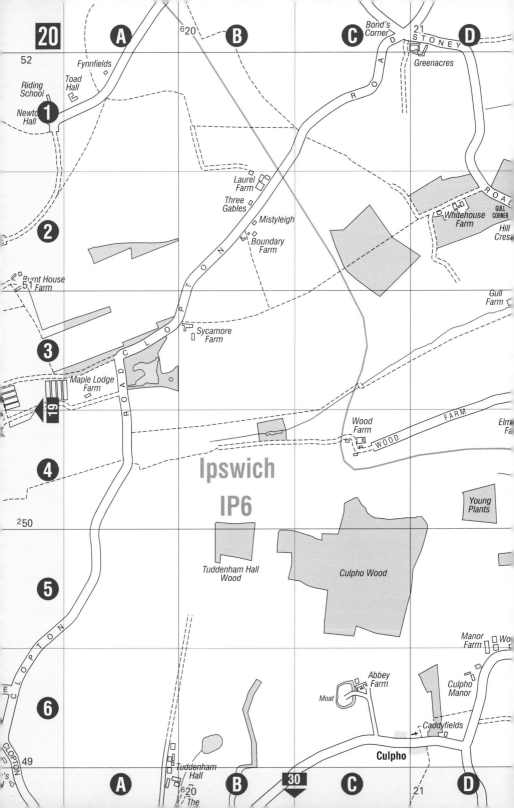

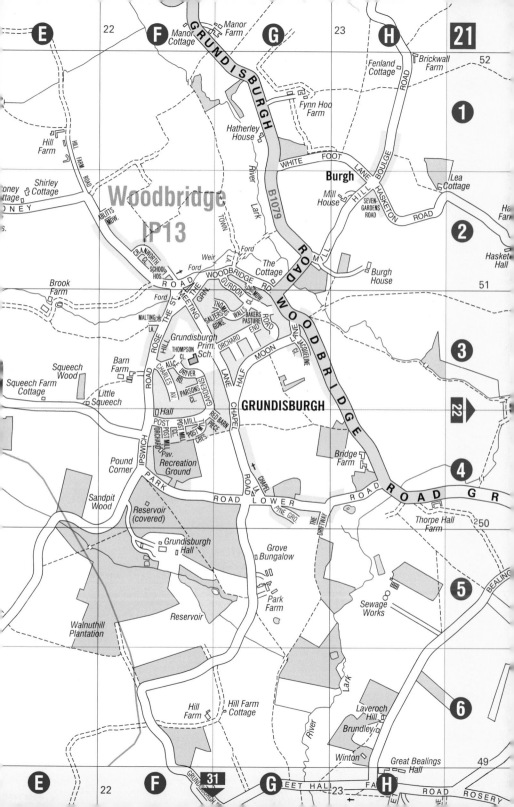

Manor Farm
Manor Cottage
GRUNDISBURGH

Fenland Cottage
Brickwall Farm
BOULGE ROAD

Manor Farm

Fynn Hoo Farm

Hatherley House

WHITE FOOT LANE

Hill Farm

HILL FARM ROAD

River Lark

B1079

Burgh

Mill House

SEVEN-GARDENS ROAD

HASKETON ROAD

Lea Cottage

Ha Far

Shirley Cottage

oney ttage

Woodbridge IP13

ABLITTS MDW.

TOWN

Weir

Ford

Ford

Ford

CRAMWORTH CL.
SCHOOL HOS.

Brook Farm

ROAD

Malting ★

THE ST.

LA.

WOODBRIDGE RD.

THE GRN.

GURDON

THOM S. SALTERS GDNS.

WALLS END

SPR MDW.

BAKERS PASTURE

ROAD

LANE

The Cottage

Ford

ROAD

Haskete Hall

Burgh House

2

51

MEETING

Grundisburgh Prim. Sch.

THOMPSON CL.

ORCHARD

MOON

LANE

JACQUELINE CL.

3

22

Squeech Wood

Barn Farm

ROSE LANE

ROAD

CHARLES RD

ALICE

DRIVER RD

PARSONS CL.

GARDENS

HALF

LANE

CHAPEL

GRUNDISBURGH

Squeech Farm Cottage

Little Squeech

Hall

POST MILL

POST MILL CL.

POST MILL CRES.

ORCHARD

Pav.

RED BARN PIECE

4

Pound Corner

IPSWICH

PARK

Recreation Ground

ROAD

LOWER

CHAPEL ROAD

PINE GRO.

THE DRIFTWAY

Bridge Farm

ROAD

GR

250

Sandpit Wood

Reservoir (covered)

Grundisburgh Hall

Grove Bungalow

Thorpe Hall Farm

Walnuthill Plantation

Reservoir

Park Farm

Sewage Works

BEALING

5

Hill Farm

Hill Farm Cottage

River Lark

Laveroch Hill

Brundley

Winton

Great Bealings Hall

ROAD ROSERY

6

49

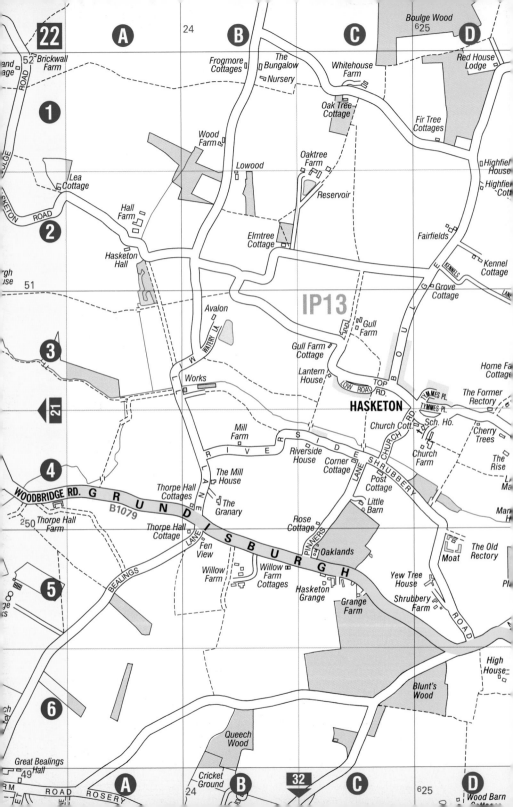

A   24   B   C   D

Boulge Wood
625

52 Brickwall
Farm

1

Frogmore
Cottages
The
Bungalow
Nursery

Whitehouse
Farm

Oak Tree
Cottage

Red House
Lodge

ROAD

Fir Tree
Cottages

Lea
Cottage

Wood
Farm

Lowood

Oaktree
Farm

Highfiel
House

KETON   ROAD

2

Hall
Farm

Reservoir

Highfie
Cott

Hasketon
Hall

Elmtree
Cottage

Fairfields

KENNELS

Kennel
Cottage

gh
se

51

IP13

Grove
Cottage

LANE

Avalon

Gull
Farm

Home Fa
Cottage

3

WATERY LA.

Works

Gull Farm
Cottage

Lantern
House

LOW ROAD

TOP
RD.

YOU

HASKETON

TYMMES PL.
TYMMES PL.

Church Cott.

Sch. Ho.

The Former
Rectory

21

Mill
Farm

RIVER

SIDE

Riverside
House

LANE

Church
Farm

Cherry
Trees

Church
Cott.

The
Rise

4

WOODBRIDGE RD.

G R U N D I

Thorpe Hall
Cottages

The Mill
House

Corner
Cottage

SHRUBBERY

Post
Cottage

CHURCH RD.

The
Ma

B1079

The
Granary

Little
Barn

250   Thorpe Hall
Farm

Thorpe Hall
Cottage

S B U R G H

Rose
Cottage

Man
H

Fen
View

Oaklands

PINNERS

The Old
Rectory

Moat

5

BEALINGS

Willow
Farm

Willow
Farm
Cottages

Hasketon
Grange

Yew Tree
House

Shrubbery
Farm

Pl

es
s

Grange
Farm

ROAD

6

High
House

Blunt's
Wood

ch

Great Bealings
Hall

49

Queech
Wood

A   ROAD   ROSERY   24   B

Cricket
Ground

32

C   625   D

Wood Barn

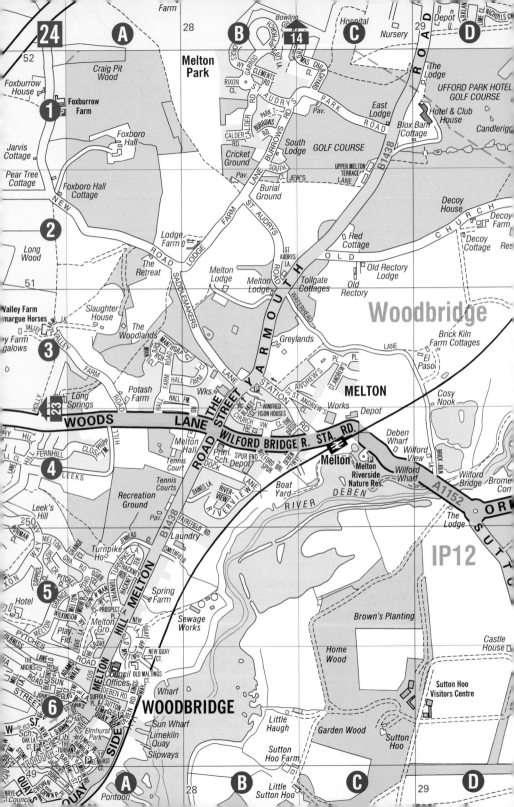

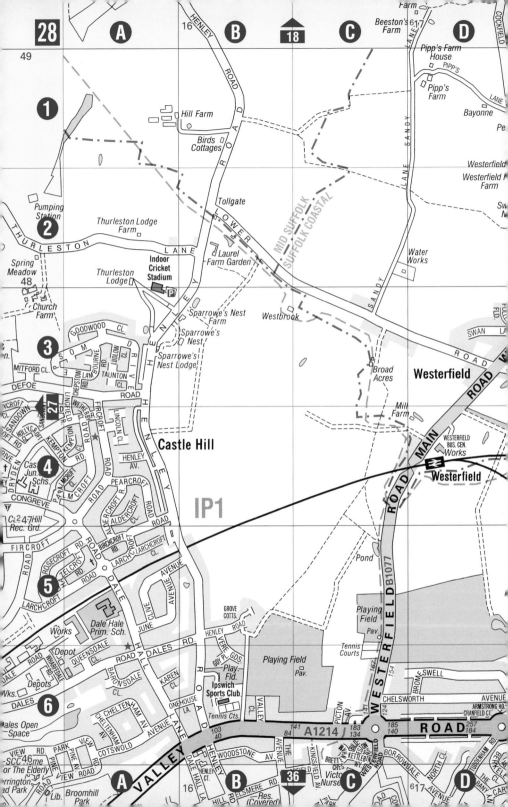

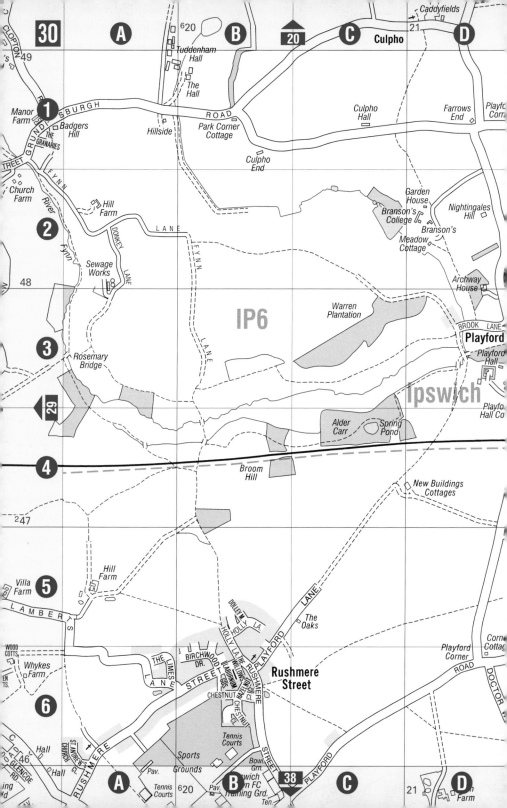

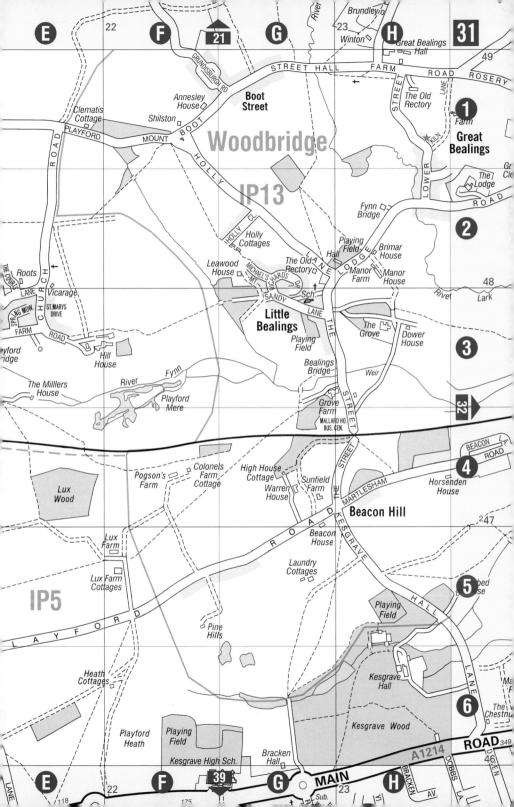

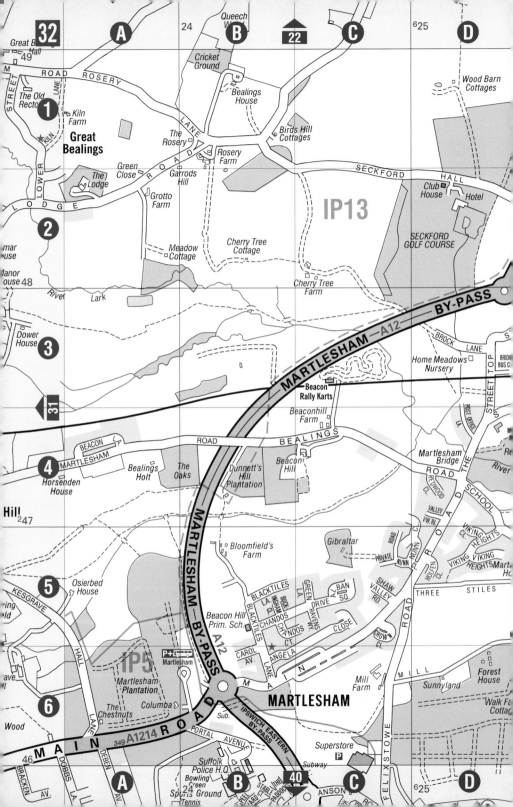

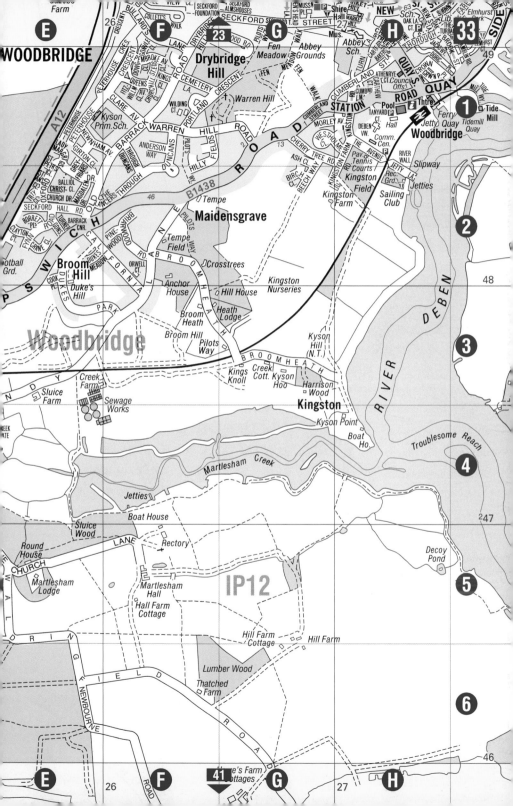

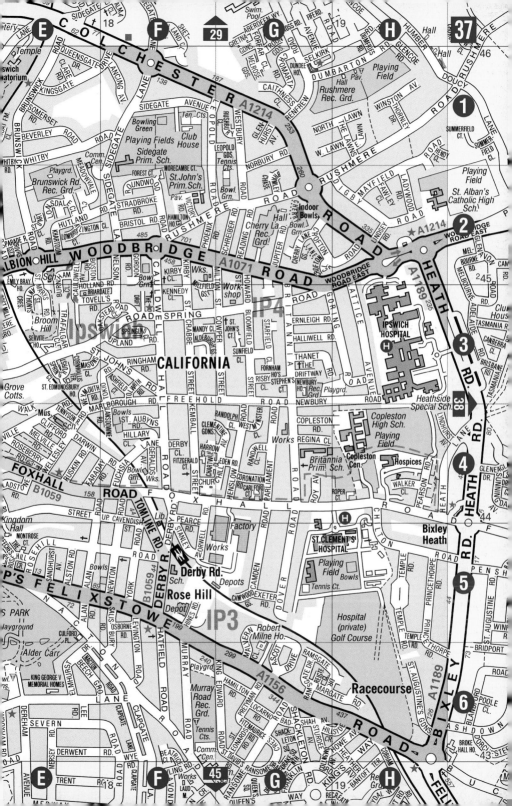

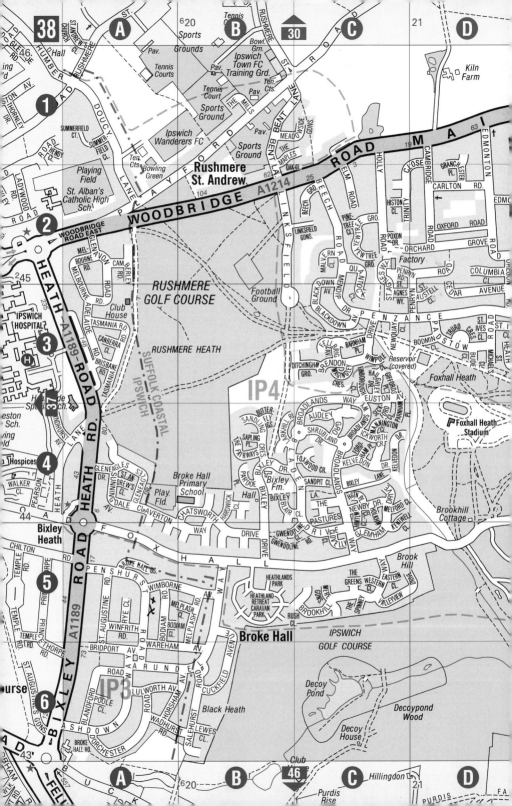

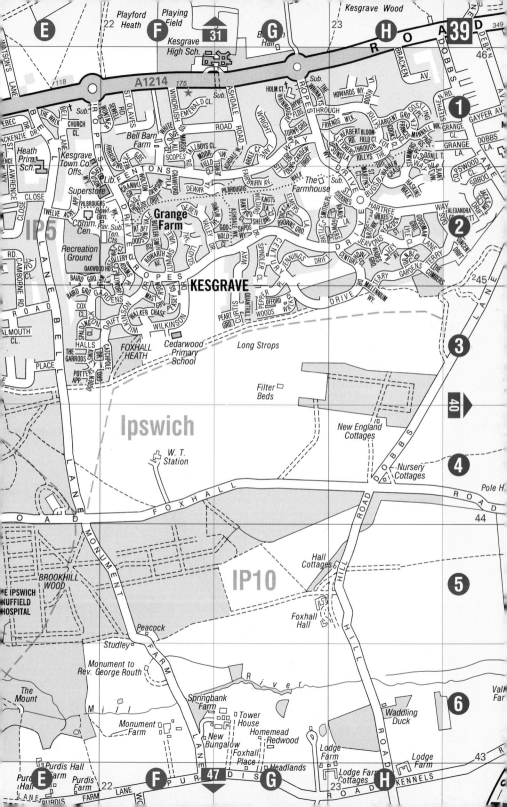

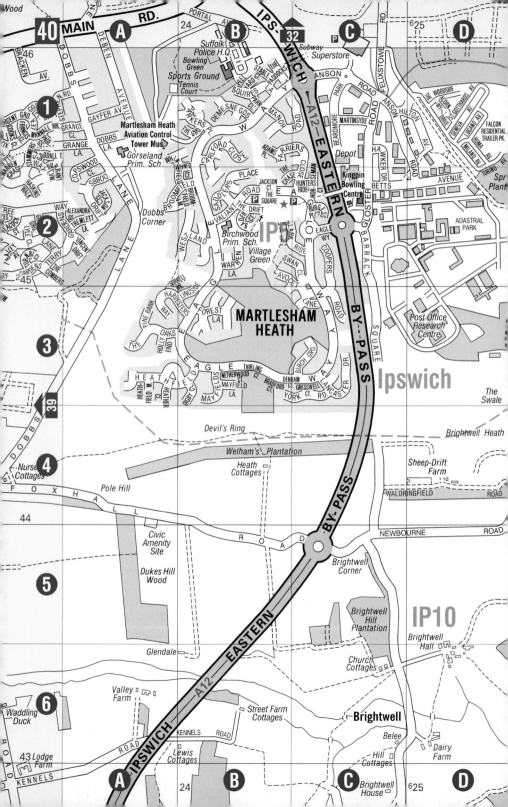

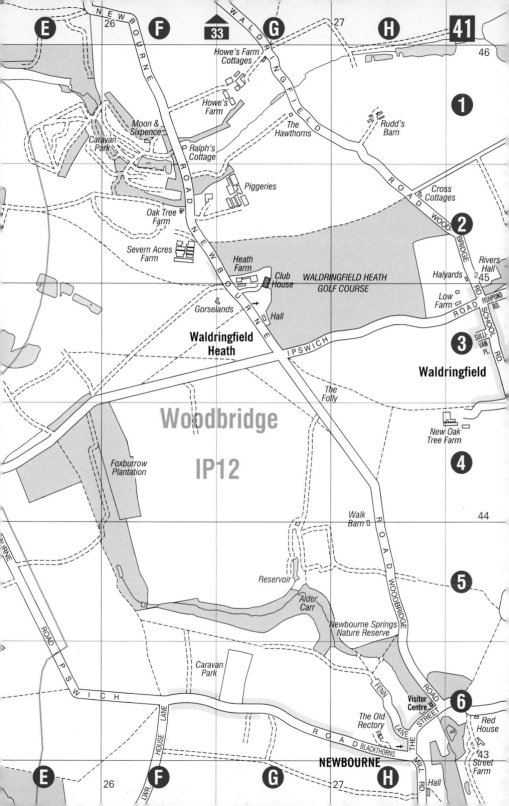

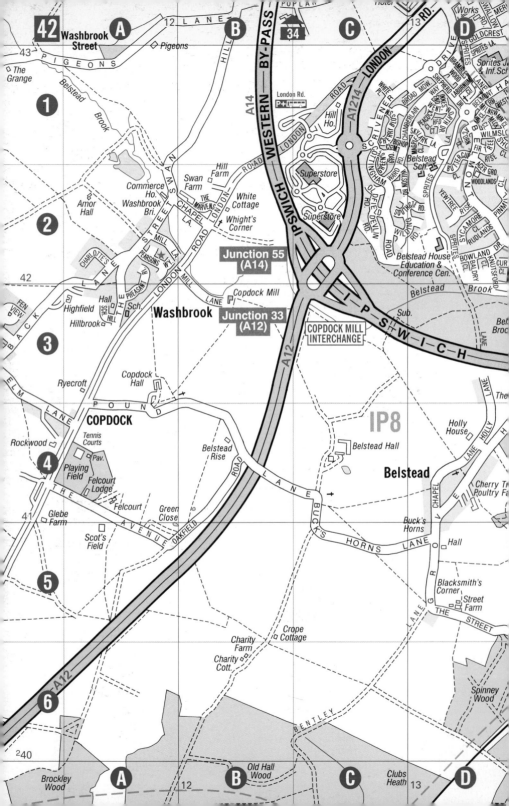

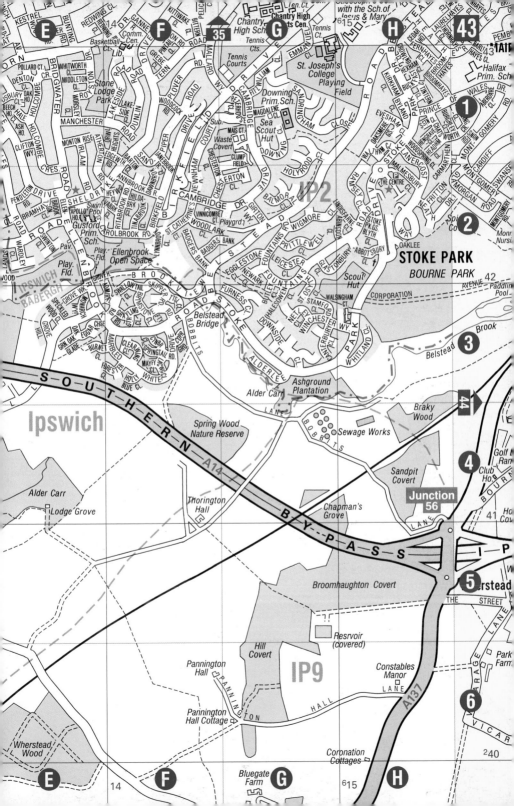

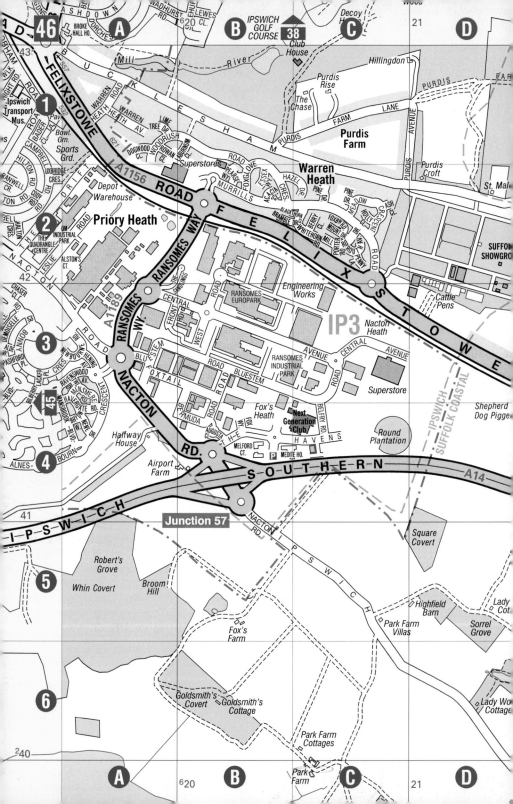

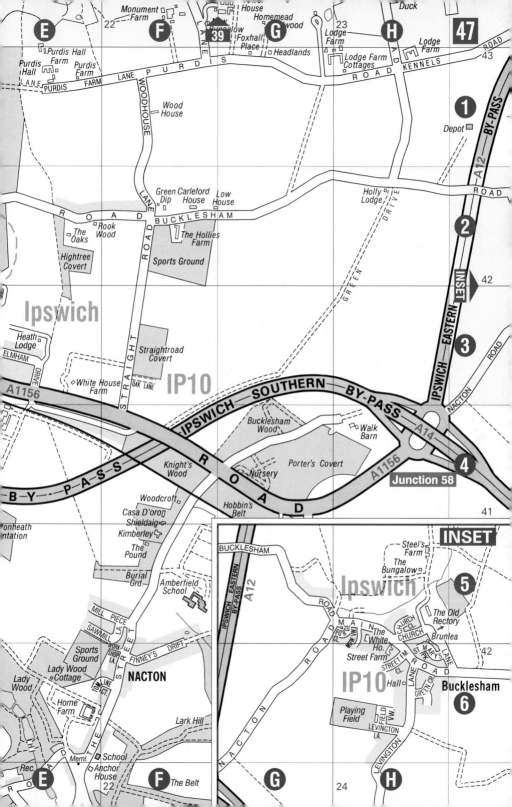

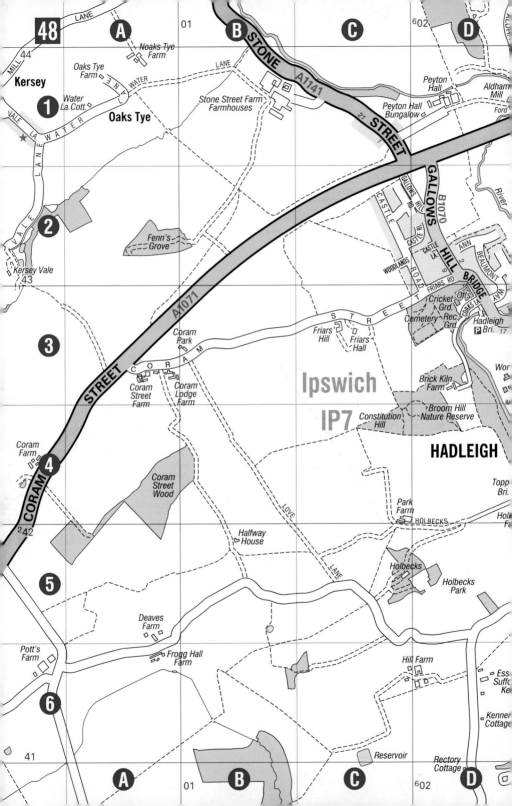

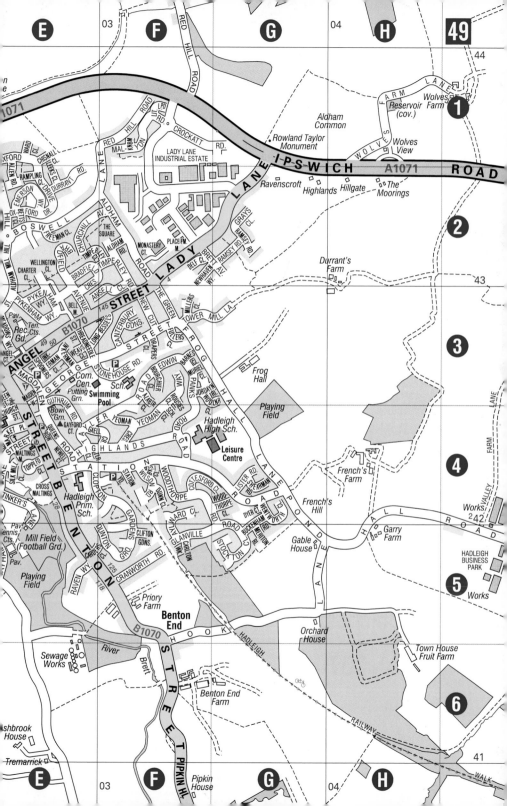

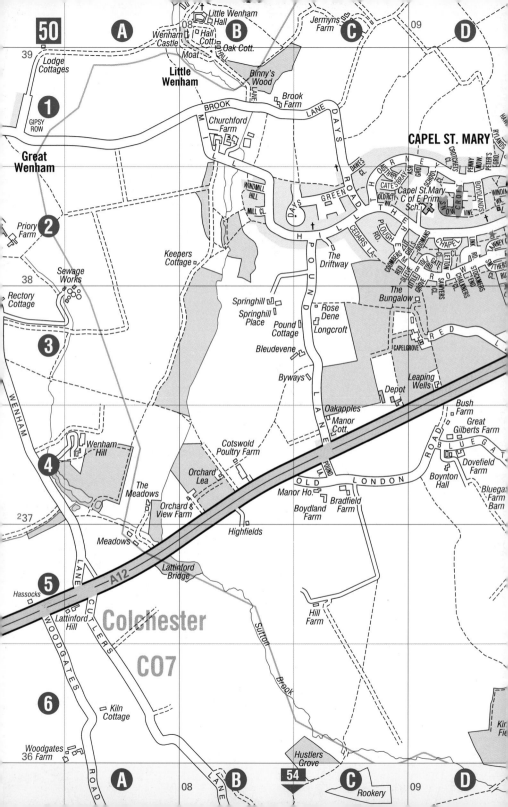

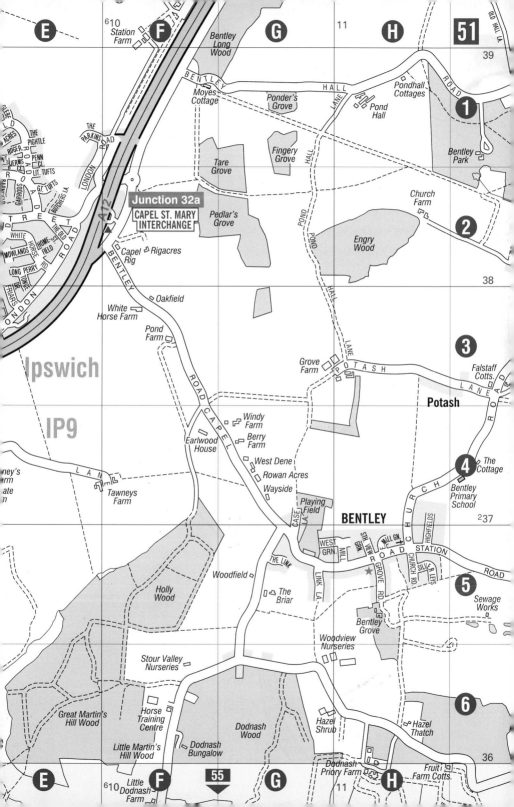

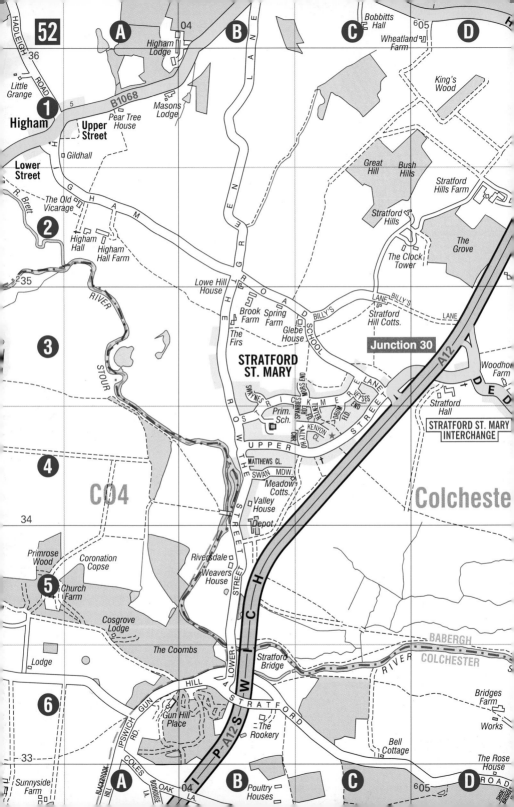

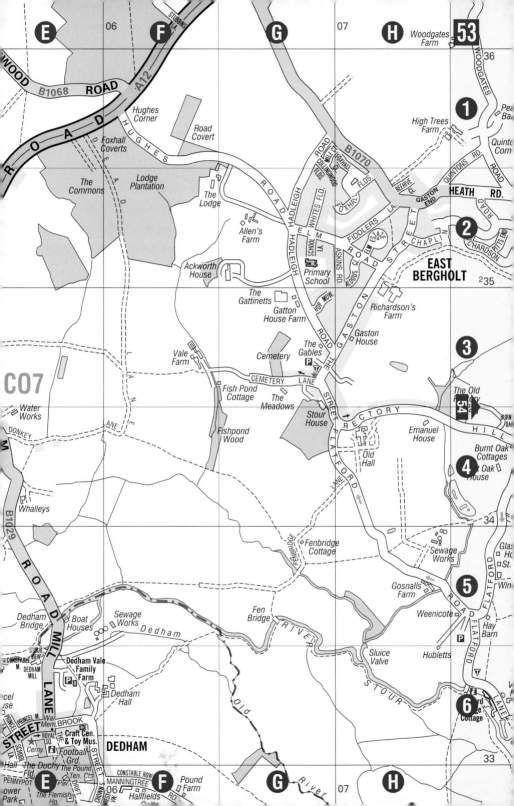

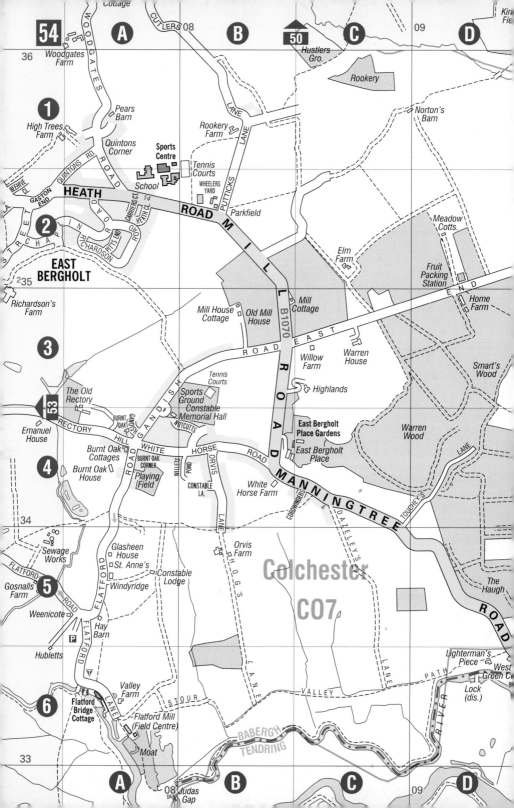

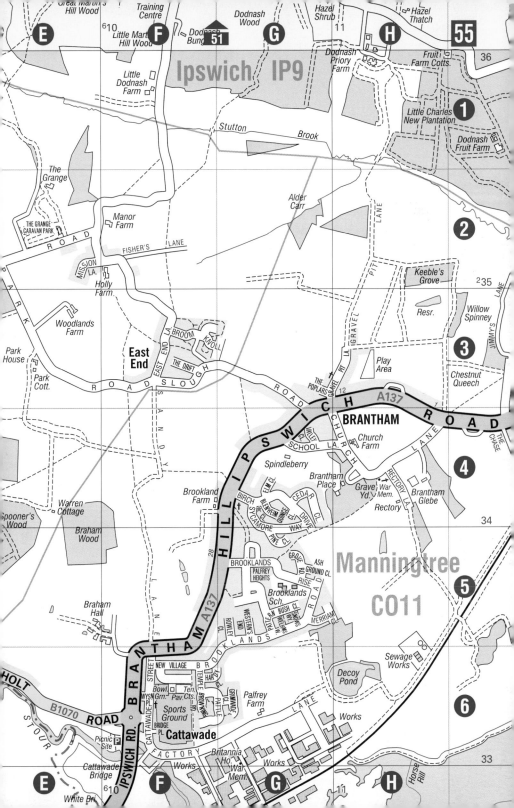

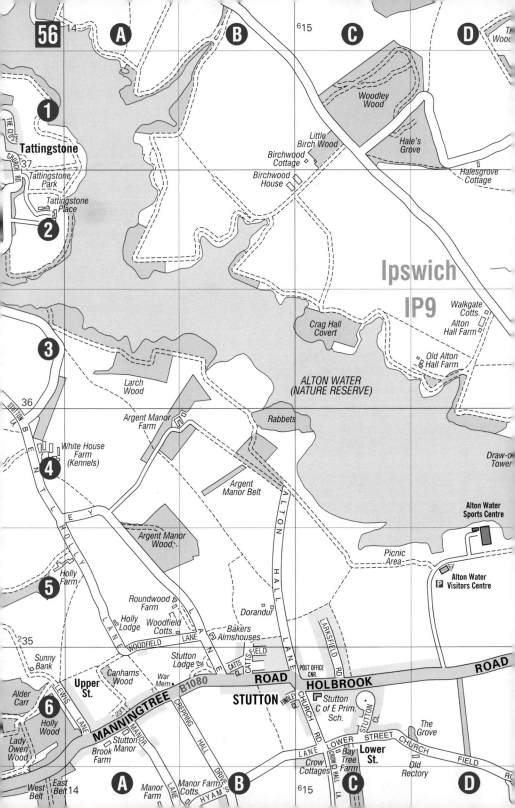

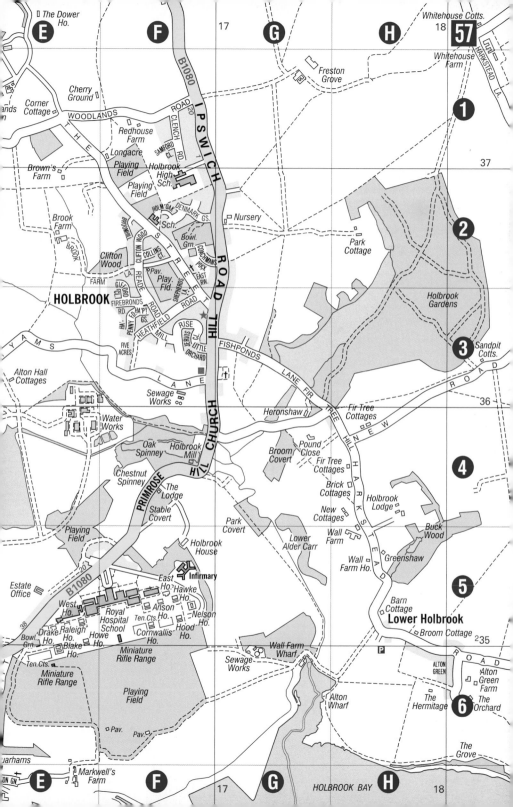

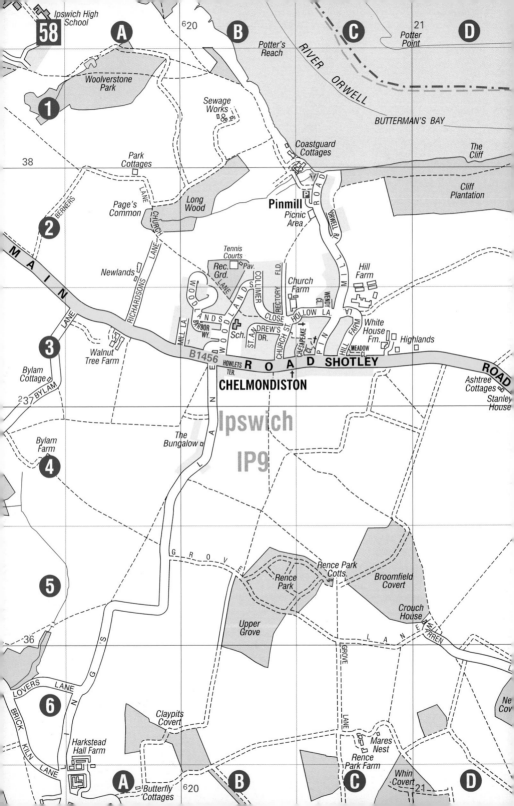

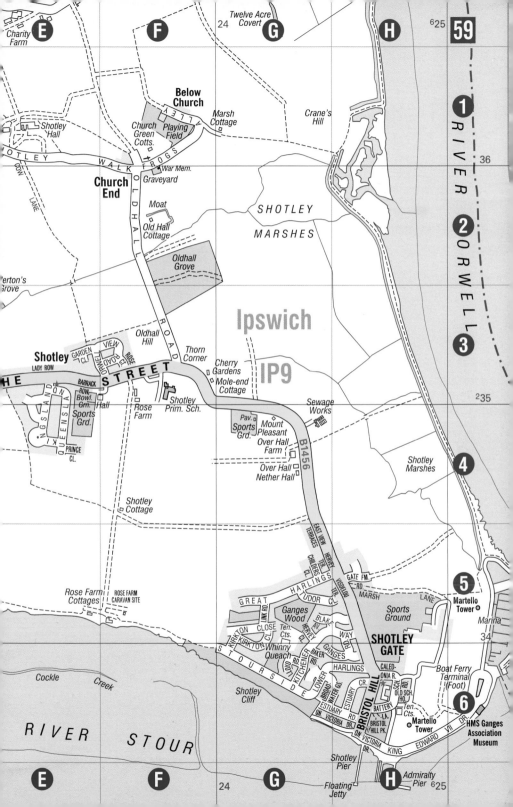

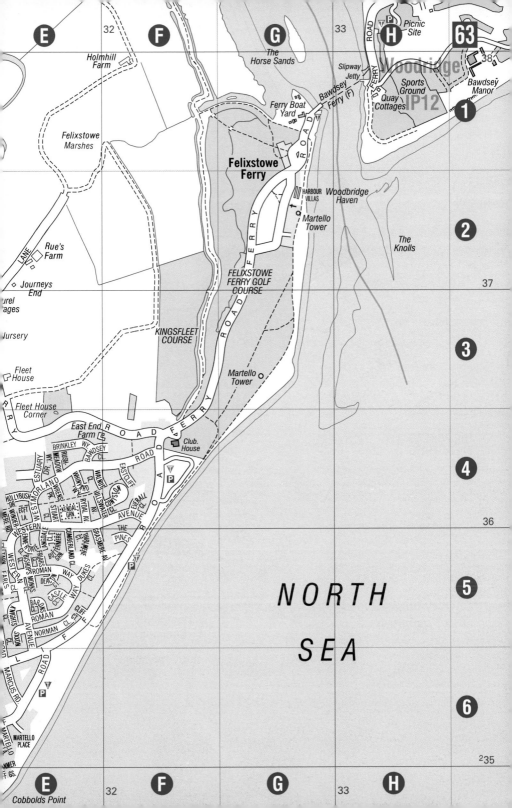

E 32 **F** **G** 33 **H** **63**

Holmhill Farm

ROAD

P Picnic Site

Woodridge

IP12

The Horse Sands

Slipway Jetty

Bawdsey Ferry (F)

FERRY

Sports Ground

Bawdsey Manor

38

1

Ferry Boat Yard

Quay Cottages

Felixstowe Marshes

ROAD

Felixstowe Ferry

HARBOUR VILLAS

Woodbridge Haven

Martello Tower

2

The Knolls

37

Rue's Farm

LANE

FERRY

FELIXSTOWE FERRY GOLF COURSE

3

Journeys End

urel ages

Jursery

KINGSFLEET COURSE

Fleet House

ROAD

Martello Tower

Fleet House Corner

East End Farm

ROAD

FERRY

ROAD

Club. House

4

BRINKLEY WY

BAWDSEY CL.

EASTCLIFF

36

ESTUARY

WESTMORLAND

HOLLYBUSH DR.

MEADOW VW.

RUSH WY.

CROFT LA.

WINDERMERE

DANDERS TER.

WALNUT CL.

ULLSWATER

RYDAL AV.

COWSLIP

KENDAL GDN.

AVENUE

THE PINES

ROAD

P

NORTH

WESTERN

NENNEY

LANGDALE

BISHOPS CL.

CUMBERLAND CL.

THIRLMERE AV.

GRASMERE AV.

ROMAN WAY

MONKS

DEANS

BUTTERMERE

WAY

DUKES CL.

CASTLE CL.

P

SEA

WRIGHTS DR.

BABB CL.

SAXON

ROMAN AVENUE

NORMAN CL.

MARCUS RD.

ROAD

P

5

6

MARTELLO PLACE

35

2

E 32 **F** **G** 33 **H**

Cobbolds Point

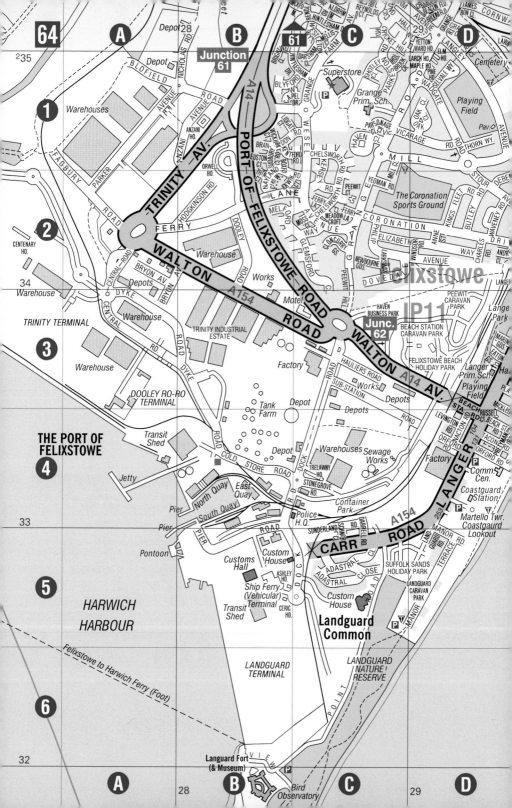

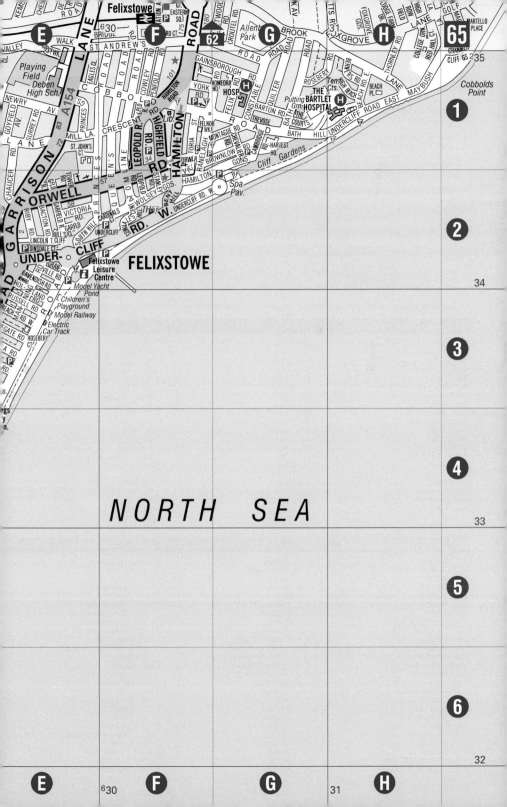

NORTH SEA

FELIXSTOWE

Felixstowe
Leisure
Centre

Model Yacht Pond
Children's Playground
Model Railway
Electric Car Track

THE BARTLET HOSPITAL

Cliff Gardens

Spa Pav.

Allenby Park

Cobbolds Point

MARTELLO PLACE

Playing Field
Deben High Sch.

E   F   G   H   65

235

1

34

2

3

4

33

5

6

32

E   630   F   G   31   H

INDEX

Including Streets, Places & Areas, Hospitals & Hospices, Industrial Estates,
Selected Flats & Walkways, Stations, Junctions and Selected Places of Interest.

HOW TO USE THIS INDEX

1. Each street name is followed by its Postcode District and then by its Locality abbreviation(s) and then by its map reference;
e.g. **Aberdeen Way** IP4: Ips . . . .6G **29** is in the IP4 Postcode District and the Ipswich Locality and is to be found in square 6G on page **29**.
The page number is shown in bold type.

2. A strict alphabetical order is followed in which Av., Rd., St., etc. (though abbreviated) are read in full and as part of the street name;
e.g. **Ash Cl.** appears after **Ashburnham Rd.** but before **Ashcroft Rd.**

3. Streets and a selection of flats and walkways too small to be shown on the maps, appear in the index with the thoroughfare to which it is
connected shown in brackets; e.g. **Adams Cl.** *IP2: Ips . . . .6B* **36** *(off Sinclair Dr.)*

4. Addresses that are in more than one part are referred to as not continuous.

5. Places and areas are shown in the index in BLUE TYPE and the map reference is to the actual map square in which the town centre or area is
located and not to the place name shown on the map; e.g. **BELSTEAD**. . . .4D **42**

6. An example of a selected place of interest is Alton Water (Nature Reserve) 3C **56**

7. An example of a station is Westerfield Station (Rail) 4D **28**

8. Junction names are shown in the index in BOLD TYPE; e.g. CAPEL ST MARY INTERCHANGE 2F **51**

9. An example of a hospital or hospice is BARTLET HOSPITAL, THE 1H **65**

10. Map references shown in brackets; e.g. **Ainslie Rd.** IP1: Ips . . . .3H **35** (1A **4**) refer to entries that also appear on the large scale pages **4-5**.

GENERAL ABBREVIATIONS

All. : Alley
App. : Approach
Av. : Avenue
Blvd. : Boulevard
Bri. : Bridge
Bus. : Business
Cvn. : Caravan
Cen. : Centre
Chu. : Church
Chyd. : Churchyard
Circ. : Circle
Cir. : Circus
Cl. : Close
Comn. : Common
Cnr. : Corner
Cotts. : Cottages
Ct. : Court
Cres. : Crescent
Cft. : Croft
Dr. : Drive
E. : East
Ent. : Enterprise

Est. : Estate
Fld. : Field
Flds. : Fields
Gdns. : Gardens
Ga. : Gate
Gt. : Great
Grn. : Green
Gro. : Grove
Hgts. : Heights
Ho. : House
Ho's. : Houses
Ind. : Industrial
Info. : Information
La. : Lane
Lit. : Little
Lwr. : Lower
Mkt. : Market
Mdw. : Meadow
Mdws. : Meadows
M. : Mews
Mt. : Mount
Mus. : Museum

Nth. : North
Pk. : Park
Pl. : Place
Res. : Residential
Ri. : Rise
Rd. : Road
Shop. : Shopping
Sth. : South
Sq. : Square
Sta. : Station
St. : Street
Ter. : Terrace
Twr. : Tower
Trad. : Trading
Up. : Upper
Va. : Vale
Vw. : View
Vs. : Villas
Vis. : Visitors
Wlk. : Walk
W. : West
Yd. : Yard

LOCALITY ABBREVIATIONS

Ake : **Akenham**
Aldh : **Aldham**
Bad : **Badley**
Barh : **Barham**
Bark : **Barking**
Baw : **Bawdsey**
Bel : **Belstead**
B'ley : **Bentley**
Bram : **Bramford**
Bran : **Brantham**
Bred : **Bredfield**
Brig : **Brightwell**
Brom : **Bromeswell**
Buc : **Bucklesham**
Burg : **Burgh**
C Ash : **Campsea Ashe**
Cap : **Capel St. Mary**
Catt : **Cattawade**
Chel : **Chelmondiston**
Cla : **Claydon**
Codd : **Coddenham**
Comb : **Combs**
Cop : **Copdock**
C Mary : **Creeting St. Mary**
C Pet : **Creeting St. Peter**

Ded : **Dedham**
E Ber : **East Bergholt**
East : **Easton**
Erw : **Erwarton**
Eyk : **Eyke**
Falk : **Falkenham**
Fel : **Felixstowe**
Fox : **Foxhall**
Fres : **Freston**
Gt Bea : **Great Bealings**
Gt Bla : **Great Blakenham**
Gt Fin : **Great Finborough**
Gt Wen : **Great Wenham**
Grun : **Grundisburgh**
Hach : **Hacheston**
Had : **Hadleigh**
Hark : **Harkstead**
Has : **Hasketon**
Hau : **Haughley**
Hen : **Henley**
High : **Higham**
Holb : **Holbrook**
Ips : **Ipswich**
Ker : **Kersey**
Kes : **Kesgrave**

L'ham : **Langham**
Law : **Lawford**
Lay : **Layham**
Leth : **Letheringham**
Lev : **Levington**
L Bea : **Little Bealings**
L Bla : **Little Blakenham**
L Wen : **Little Wenham**
L Hac : **Lower Hacheston**
Mart : **Martlesham**
Mart H : **Martlesham Heath**
Mel : **Melton**
Nac : **Nacton**
N Mar : **Needham Market**
New : **Newbourne**
O New : **Old Newton**
One : **Onehouse**
Pett : **Pettistree**
Play : **Playford**
Pur F : **Purdis Farm**
Rus A : **Rushmere St. Andrew**
S'ly : **Shotley**
S Gate : **Shotley Gate**
Spro : **Sproughton**
S'ket : **Stowmarket**

S'and : **Stowupland**
Stra M : **Stratford St. Mary**
Sutt : **Sutton**
Swil : **Swilland**
Tatt : **Tattingstone**
T Mart : **Trimley St. Martin**

T Mary : **Trimley St. Mary**
Tudd : **Tuddenham**
Uff : **Ufford**
Wald : **Waldringfield**
Wash : **Washbrook**
West : **Westerfield**

Wher : **Wherstead**
W Mar : **Wickham Market**
Wit : **Witnesham**
Wol : **Wolverstone**
Wood : **Woodbridge**

A

Abbotsbury Cl. IP2: Ips 2H **43**
Abbot's Hall Rd. IP14: S'ket 6D **6**
Abbot's Wlk. IP14: S'ket 6D **6**
Aberdare Cl. IP2: Ips 1A **44**
Aberdeen Way IP4: Ips 6G **29**
Aberfoyle Cl. IP4: Ips 6H **29**
Abingdon Cl. IP2: Ips 2H **43**
Ablitts Mdw. IP13: Grun 2F **21**
Acacia Cl. IP3: Pur F 2B **46**
Acer Gro. IP2: Ips 2D **42**
Acorn Cl. IP2: Ips 1D **42**
Acorn Way IP5: Mart H 1D **40**
Acre Cl. IP6: Wit 1F **19**
Acton Cl. IP8: Bram 5B **26**
Acton Gdns. IP8: Bram 5B **26**
Acton Rd. IP8: Bram 5B **26**
Adair Rd. IP1: Ips 1E **35**
Adams Cl. *IP2: Ips* 6B **36**
(off Sinclair Dr.)
Adams Pl. IP5: Kes 2F **39**
Adams Wlk. IP12: Wood 6A **24**
Adastral Cl. IP11: Fel 5C **64**
Adastral Pk. IP5: Mart H 2D **40**
Addington Rd. IP11: T Mary 4F **61**
Addison Way IP6: Gt Bla 5A **16**
Adelaide Rd. IP4: Ips 3A **38**
Admiral Rd. IP3: Ips 3F **43**
Admirals Wlk. IP12: Wood 4G **23**
Agate Cl. IP1: Ips 6E **27**
Ainslie Rd. IP1: Ips 3H **35** (1A **4**)
Aisthorpe IP9: Cap 2C **50**
AKENHAM 1G **27**
Alabaster Cl. IP7: Had 3F **49**
Alan Rd. IP3: Ips 5E **37**
Alasdair Pl. IP6: Cla 5D **16**
Alban Sq. IP12: Mart 5C **32**
Albany, The IP4: Ips 1D **36**
Alberta Cl. IP5: Kes 1D **38**
Albert Wlk. *IP11: Fel* 1F **65**
(off Victoria St.)
Albion Hill IP4: Ips 2E **37**
Albion Wharf IP3: Ips 4E **5**
Aldeburgh Gdns. IP4: Ips 3F **37**
Alder Carr Farm 3E **11**
Aldercroft Cl. IP1: Ips 4A **28**
Aldercroft Rd. IP1: Ips 5A **28**
Alderlee IP2: Ips 3G **43**
Alderman Rd. IP1: Ips 4A **36** (2A **4**)
Aldham Gdns. IP14: S'ket 1E **9**
Aldham Mill Hill IP7: Had 1D **48**
Aldham Rd. IP7: Had 2F **49**
Aldis Av. IP14: S'ket 1D **8**
Aldous Cl. CO7: E Ber 2H **53**
Aldringham M. IP11: Fel 6G **61**
Alexander Dr. IP6: N Mar 3C **10**
Alexandra Gdns. IP5: Kes 2A **40**
Alexandra Rd. IP4: Ips 3D **36** (1H **5**)
IP11: Fel 5H **61**
Alice Driver Rd. IP13: Grun 3F **21**
Allenby Rd. IP2: Ips 3G **35**
Allen Rd. IP7: Had 2E **49**
All Fired Up Ceramics *2C* **4**
(off Tower Ramparts)
Allhallows Ct. IP3: Ips 2F **45**
Allington Cl. IP4: Ips 2E **37**
All Saints' Rd. IP1: Ips 1H **35**
Alma Cl. IP4: Ips 6F **29**
Almondhayes IP2: Ips 1H **35**
Alnesbourn Cres. IP3: Ips 4H **45**
Alpe St. IP1: Ips 2A **36**
Alston Rd. IP3: Ips 5E **37**
Alston's Ct. IP3: Ips 2A **46**
Alton Grn. IP9: Holb 6H **57**
Alton Hall La. IP9: Sutt 4B **56**

Alton Water (Nature Reserve) 3C **56**
Alton Water Sports Cen. 4D **56**
Alton Water Vis. Cen. 5D **56**
Alvis Wlk. IP1: Ips 6D **26**
America Hill IP6: Wit 3F **19**
Ancaster Rd. IP2: Ips 5A **36** (5A **4**)
Anchor St. IP3: Ips 6G **5**
Ancient House 2D **4**
Anderson Cl. IP6: N Mar 3C **10**
Anderson Way IP12: Wood 1F **33**
Andrew Cl. IP11: Fel 2D **64**
Andros Cl. IP2: Ips 4F **45**
Angela Cl. IP12: Mart 6B **32**
Angel Ct. IP7: Had 3E **49**
Angel La. IP2: Ips 4C **36** (4F **5**)
IP12: Wood 6H **23**
Angel Rd. IP8: Bram 5B **26**
Angel St. IP7: Had 3E **49**
Anglesea Rd. IP1: Ips 2H **35**
Anglia Kart Racing 1D **34**
Anglia Parkway Nth. IP1: Ips 3E **27**
Anglia Parkway Sth. IP1: Ips 3E **27**
Anglia Sporting Activities 3B **14**
Angus Cl. IP4: Ips 6G **29**
Anita Cl. E. IP2: Ips 4F **35**
Anita Cl. W. IP2: Ips 4F **35**
Ann Beaumont Way IP7: Had 2D **48**
Annbrook Rd. IP2: Ips 2F **43**
Anne St. IP11: Fel 2D **64**
Ann St. IP1: Ips 2A **36** (1A **4**)
Ansell Cl. IP7: Had 3E **49**
Anson Rd. IP5: Mart H 1C **40**
Anthonys Cres. IP4: Ips 3E **37**
Antrim Rd. IP1: Ips 6E **27**
Anzani Av. IP11: Fel 1B **64**
Anzani Rd. IP11: Fel 1B **64**
Apollo Ho. IP2: Ips 2E **43**
Appleby Cl. IP2: Ips 2D **42**
Arcade St. IP1: Ips 3B **36** (2C **4**)
Archangel Gdns. IP2: Ips 5F **35**
Arches, The IP12: Wood 6H **23**
Argyle St. IP4: Ips 3C **36** (2F **5**)
Arkle Ct. IP5: Kes 1G **39**
Arkwright Rd. IP2: Ips 3F **35**
Armstrong Ho. IP4: Ips 6D **28**
Arnold Cl. IP11: Fel 4G **27**
Arras Sq. IP1: Ips 2D **4**
Arthur's Ter. IP1: Ips 3D **36** (2G **5**)
Arundel Way IP3: Ips 6A **38**
Arwela Rd. IP11: Fel 3E **65**
Ascot Dr. IP3: Ips 6G **37**
IP11: Fel 5H **61**
Ashbocking Rd. IP6: Hen 2A **18**
Ashburnham Rd. IP6: N Mar 4C **10**
Ash Cl. IP3: Pur F 2C **46**
IP12: Wood 1G **33**
Ashcroft Rd. IP1: Ips 6G **27**
Ashdale Rd. IP5: Kes 1G **39**
Ashdale Wlk. IP5: Kes 1G **39**
(Fentons Way, not continuous)
IP5: Kes 2G **39**
(Ropes Dr.)
Ashdown Way IP3: Ips 6A **38**
Ashfield Ct. IP4: Ips 3F **37**
Ash Ground Cl. CO11: Bran 5G **55**
Ashground Ct. IP11: T Mart 1E **61**
Ash Gro. IP9: Cap 2D **50**
Ash Ho. IP2: Ips 1E **43**
Ashley Ho. IP11: Fel 5B **64**
Ashley St. IP2: Ips 5B **36** (6D **4**)
Ashmere Gro. IP4: Ips 3E **37** (1H **5**)
Ash Rd. IP13: L Hac 3G **13**
(not continuous)
Ashton Cl. IP2: Ips 1D **42**
Askins Rd. CO7: E Ber 2H **53**
Aspen Cl. IP6: Gt Bla 3A **16**
IP12: Mel 5A **24**

Aspley Ct. *IP1: Ips* 2H **35**
(off Wellington St.)
Aster Rd. IP2: Ips 6F **35**
Aston Cl. IP1: Ips 6D **26**
Ataka Rd. IP11: Fel 5A **62**
Athenrye Ct. IP12: Wood 1H **33**
Atherton Rd. IP2: Ips 1E **43**
Athroll M. *IP5: Kes* 1H **39**
(off Booth La.)
Atlas Ho. IP4: Ips 2F **5**
Audley Gro. IP4: Rus A 4C **38**
Augusta Cl. IP3: Ips 4B **46**
Austin St. IP2: Ips 5B **36** (5D **4**)
Avenswood Av. IP3: Ips 3G **45**
Avenue, The IP1: Ips 6B **28**
IP8: Cop 4A **42**
IP11: T Mary 4E **61**
IP12: Wood 1H **33**
IP13: Uff 6D **14**
Avocet Ct. IP11: Fel 2D **64**
Avocet La. IP5: Mart H 2B **40**
Avondale Rd. IP3: Ips 1F **45**
Aylward Cl. IP7: Had 5F **49**
Ayr Rd. IP4: Ips 5G **29**

B

Back Hamlet IP3: Ips 4D **36** (4G **5**)
Back La. IP6: Cla 5D **16**
IP8: Wash 3A **42**
IP10: Falk 1B **62**
IP11: Fel 6A **62**
Bacon Rd. IP6: Barh, Cla 4D **16**
Bacton Rd. IP11: Fel 2E **65**
Baden Powell Wlk. *IP5: Kes* 2H **39**
(off Hartree Way)
Bader Cl. IP3: Ips 1H **45**
Bader Ct. IP5: Mart H 2B **40**
Badgers Bank IP2: Ips 2F **43**
Badley Hill IP6: Bad 1B **10**
Badley La. IP6: Bad 5G **9**
IP14: Bad, Comb 5E **9**
Badley Wlk. IP6: Bad 5F **9**
Badshah Av. IP3: Ips 6G **37**
Bailey Av. IP5: Kes 2H **39**
Bailey Cl. IP2: Ips 3F **35**
Baird Cl. IP2: Ips 2G **35**
Baird Gro. IP5: Kes 2E **39**
Baker Rd. IP9: S Gate 6G **59**
Bakers La. IP12: Wood 1H **33**
Bakers Pasture IP13: Grun 3G **21**
Baldry Cl. IP8: Ips 2D **42**
Baldwin Rd. IP14: S'ket 1C **8**
Ballater Cl. IP1: Ips 3F **27**
Balliol Cl. IP12: Wood 2E **33**
Balmoral Cl. IP2: Ips 2G **43**
Bank Rd. IP4: Ips 3D **36** (1H **5**)
Banks Cl. IP7: Had 4F **49**
Bantoft Ter. IP3: Ips 1H **45**
Banyard Cl. IP5: Kes 2G **39**
BARHAM 2F **17**
Barham Chu. La. IP6: Barh 3D **16**
BARHAM GREEN 1G **17**
Barhams Way IP13: W Mar 4F **13**
Barker Cl. IP2: Ips 4E **35**
Barking Rd. IP6: N Mar 5D **10**
Barleyhayes Cl. IP2: Ips 1A **44**
Barnes Cl. IP7: Had 3F **49**
Barnfield IP9: Cap 2E **51**
IP11: Fel 5G **61**
Barnham Pl. IP5: Rus A 3C **38**
Barons Ct. IP11: Fel 5E **63**
Baronsdale Cl. IP1: Ips 6A **28**
Barrack Cnr. IP1: Ips 3A **36** (1B **4**)
IP12: Wood 2E **33**

Barrack La. IP1: Ips 3A **36** (1B **4**)
IP13: Uff 6E **15**
Barrack Row IP9: S'ly 3E **59**
Barrack Sq. IP5: Mart H 2C **40**
Barrett's La. IP6: N Mar 4B **10**
Bartholomew St. IP1: Ips 3E **37** (2H **5**)
BARTLET HOSPITAL, THE 1H **65**
Barton Cl. IP2: Ips 1F **43**
Barton Rd. IP11: Fel 1G **65**
IP12: Wood 4G **23**
Bartrum La. IP5: Kes 2F **39**
Bath Hill IP11: Fel 1G **65**
Bath Rd. IP11: Fel 1G **65**
Bath St. IP2: Ips 6C **36** (6E **5**)
Battery La. IP9: S Gate 6H **59**
Battles La. IP5: Kes 2G **39**
Bawdsey Cl. IP11: Fel 4E **63**
Beach Pl. IP11: Fel 1H **65**
Beach Rd. E. IP11: Fel 1H **65**
Beach Rd. W. IP11: Fel 3E **65**
Beach Sta. Cvn. Pk. IP11: Fel 3C **64**
Beach Sta. Rd. IP11: Fel 3D **64**
Beacon Fld. IP11: Fel 6H **61**
BEACON HILL 4H **31**
Beacon La. IP13: L Bea 4A **32**
Beacon Rally Karts 3C **32**
Beaconsfield Rd. IP1: Ips 2G **35**
IP12: Wood 6H **23**
Bealings La. IP13: Has 5A **22**
Bealings Rd. IP12: Mart 4C **32**
Beardmore Pk. IP5: Mart H 1C **40**
Beatrice Av. IP11: Fel 5B **62**
Beatrice Cl. IP3: Ips 6F **37**
Beatty Rd. IP3: Ips 1G **45**
Beaufort Pl. IP1: Ips 2H **35**
(off Beaufort St.)
Beaufort St. IP1: Ips 2H **35**
Beaumont Way IP14: S'ket 6B **6**
Becketts, The IP14: S'ket 3B **6**
Bedford St. IP1: Ips 3A **36** (1B **4**)
Beech Cl. IP8: Spro 3B **34**
Beechcroft Rd. IP1: Ips 6G **27**
Beeches, The IP3: Ips 5E **37** (5H **5**)
IP6: Cla .5D **16**
Beech Gro. IP3: Ips 6E **37**
IP5: Rus A 2C **38**
Beech Ho. IP2: Ips 1E **43**
Beech Rd. IP5: Rus A 2C **38**
Beech Ter. IP14: S'ket 4D **6**
Beech Way IP12: Wood 2G **33**
Beehive Cl. CO7: E Ber 2H **53**
Belgrave Cl. IP4: Ips 6D **28**
Bell Cl. IP2: Ips 5B **36** (5D **4**)
Belle Vue Rd. IP4: Ips 3D **36** (1H **5**)
Bell La. IP2: Ips 5B **36** (5D **4**)
IP5: Kes .1E **39**
Bell M. IP7: Had 3E **49**
Bell's Cross Rd. IP6: Barh 1F **17**
Belmont Rd. IP2: Ips 1D **42**
IP8: Ips .1D **42**
BELOW CHURCH 1F **59**
BELSTEAD 4D **42**
Belstead Av. IP2: Ips 6A **36** (6B **4**)
Belstead Rd. IP2: Ips 2F **43** (6A **4**)
Belvedere Rd. IP4: Ips 1D **36**
Benacre Rd. IP3: Ips 1F **45**
Benezet St. IP1: Ips 3A **36** (1A **4**)
Bennett Rd. IP1: Ips 1E **35**
Bent Hill IP11: Fel 2F **65**
Bent La. IP4: Rus A 1B **38**
BENTLEY 5H **51**
Bentley Hall Rd. IP9: Cap, B'ley 1F **51**
Bentley La. IP8: Bel 6C **42**
IP9: Sutt 4A **56**
Bentley Rd. IP1: Ips 5D **26**
IP9: Cap .2F **51**
BENTON END 5F **49**
Benton St. IP7: Had 4E **49**
Beresford Dr. IP12: Wood 4G **23**
Bergholt Rd. CO11: Bran 6E **55**
Berkeley Cl. IP4: Ips 6D **28**
Bermuda Rd. IP3: Ips 4B **46**
Bernard Cres. IP3: Ips 1G **45**
Berners La. IP9: Chel 2A **58**
Berners Rd. IP11: Fel 1H **65**
Berners St. IP1: Ips 3A **36** (1B **4**)

Berry Cl. IP3: Pur F 2C **46**
Betts Av. IP5: Mart H 2C **40**
Betts Cl. IP7: Had 2E **49**
Beverley Ct. IP4: Ips 1F **5**
Beverley Rd. IP4: Ips 1E **37**
Bibb Way IP1: Ips 4H **35** (3A **4**)
Bilberry Rd. IP3: Ips 3H **45**
Bildeston Gdns. IP4: Ips 6C **28**
Bildeston Rd. IP14: Comb 5A **8**
Billy's La. CO7: Stra M 3C **52**
Bilney Rd. IP12: Wood 6F **23**
Birch Cl. IP12: Wood 2G **33**
IP13: W Mar 5F **13**
IP14: S'and 3G **7**
Bishop M. IP8: Ips 1C **42**
Bishops Cl. IP11: Fel 6G **61**
Bishopsgarth IP3: Ips 5E **37** (5H **5**)
Bishop's Hill IP3: Ips 5D **36** (5H **5**)
Bittern Cl. IP2: Ips 6F **35**
Bixley Dr. IP4: Rus A 4B **38**
BIXLEY HEATH 4H **37**
Bixley La. IP4: Rus A 4B **38**
(not continuous)
Bixley Rd. IP3: Ips 6H **37**
Black Arches IP8: Ips 3F **43**
(off Ellenbrook Rd.)
Black Barns IP11: T Mary 4F **61**
Blackbird Way IP14: S'ket 5G **7**
Blackbrook Hill
CO7: Ded, L'ham 6A **52**
Blackdown Av. IP5: Rus A 3C **38**
Blackfriars Ct. IP1: Ips 4C **36** (3E **5**)
Black Horse La. IP1: Ips 3A **36** (1B **4**)
Black Horse Wlk. IP1: Ips 2C **4**
Blackthorn Cl. IP3: Pur F 2B **46**
Blackthorns IP12: New 6H **41**
Blacktiles La. IP12: Mart 5B **32**
Bladen Dr. IP4: Rus A 4B **38**
Blair Cl. IP4: Rus A 4B **38**
Blake Av. IP9: S Gate 5G **59**
Blake Rd. IP1: Ips 4G **27**
IP14: S'ket 4B **6**
Blakes Cl. IP12: Mel 4B **24**
Blanche St. IP4: Ips 3C **36** (2F **5**)
Blandford Rd. IP3: Ips 6A **38**
Blenheim Cl. CO11: Bran 4G **55**
Blenheim Ct. IP1: Ips 2H **35**
(off Beaufort St.)
Blenheim Rd. IP1: Ips 2H **35**
Blickling Cl. IP2: Ips 1A **44**
Blofield Rd. IP11: Fel 1A **64**
Bloomfield Cl. IP5: Kes 1H **39**
Bloomfield St. IP4: Ips 3G **37**
Blue Barn Cl. IP11: T Mart 1D **60**
Blue Barn La. IP6: Gt Bla 5A **16**
Bluebell Cl. IP2: Ips 5F **35**
Bluebell Gro. IP6: N Mar 5D **10**
Bluegate La. IP9: Cap 4D **50**
Blueleighs Cvn. Pk. IP6: Gt Bla 3A **16**
Bluestem Rd. IP3: Ips 3A **46**
Blyford Way IP11: Fel 1B **64**
Blyth Cl. IP2: Ips 2H **43**
Boat Ferry Terminal (Foot) 6H **59**
Boatman Cl. IP8: Ips 3F **43**
(off Marbled White Dr.)
Bobbits La. IP8: Ips 3F **43**
Bodiam Cl. IP3: Ips 5A **38**
Bodiam Rd. IP3: Ips 5A **38**
Bodmin Cl. IP5: Kes 3D **38**
Bolton La. IP4: Ips 3C **36** (1E **5**)
Bond St. IP4: Ips 4C **36** (3F **5**)
IP14: S'ket 4D **6**
Bonnington Rd. IP3: Ips 2E **45**
Booth La. IP5: Kes 1H **39**
BOOT STREET 1F **31**
Boot St. IP13: Gt Bea 1F **31**
Border Cot La. IP13: W Mar 4F **13**
Borrett Cl. IP12: Wood 2E **33**

Borrowdale Av. IP4: Ips 6C **28**
Bosmere Ct. IP6: N Mar 4D **10**
Boss Hall Bus. Pk. IP1: Ips 2F **35**
Boss Hall Rd. IP1: Ips 2F **35**
Bostock Rd. IP2: Ips 2B **44**
Boston Rd. IP4: Ips 2E **37**
Boswell La. IP7: Had 2E **49**
Boulge Rd. IP13: Burg 1H **21**
IP13: Has 3C **22**
Boulters Cl. IP14: S'ket 5B **6**
Boulters Way IP14: S'ket 5B **6**
Bourchier Cl. IP7: Had 3F **49**
Bourne Hill IP2: Wher 4A **44**
Bourne Pk. Res. Pk.
IP2: Ips .2A **44**
Bourne Ter. IP2: Wher 3A **44**
Bowland Dr. IP8: Ips 2D **42**
Bowthorpe Cl. IP1: Ips 2A **36**
Boxford Cl. IP14: S'ket 2E **9**
Boxford Ct. IP11: Fel 1B **64**
Boxhouse La. CO7: Ded 6A **52**
(not continuous)
Boydlands IP9: Cap 2D **50**
Boyton Hall Dr. IP14: S'ket 2A **8**
Boyton Rd. IP3: Ips 3G **45**
Bracken Av. IP5: Kes 1H **39**
Brackenbury Cl. IP1: Ips 1A **36**
Brackenbury Sports Cen. 6D **62**
Brackenhayes Cl. IP2: Ips 6A **36**
Brackley Cl. IP11: Fel 6G **61**
Bradfield Av. IP7: Had 2E **49**
Bradfield Cres. IP7: Had 2E **49**
Bradford Ct. IP5: Mart H 3B **40**
Bradley St. IP2: Ips 5B **36** (6D **4**)
Bramble Dr. IP3: Pur F 2B **46**
Bramblewood IP8: Ips 1D **42**
BRAMFORD .5B **26**
Bramford La. IP1: Ips 6E **27**
Bramford Rd. IP1: Ips 1D **34** (1A **4**)
IP6: Gt Bla 4A **16**
IP8: Bram 6D **26**
Bramhall Cl. IP2: Ips 2E **43**
Bramley Chase IP4: Ips 2G **37**
Brandon Rd. IP11: Fel 1B **64**
Bransby Gdns. IP4: Ips 2D **36**
BRANTHAM .4G **55**
Brantham Hill CO11: Catt, Bran 6F **55**
Brantham Mill Ind. Est CO11: Bran 6D **54**
Brazier's Wood Rd. IP3: Ips 3G **45**
Brecon Cl. IP2: Ips 1A **44**
Bredfield Cl. IP11: Fel 6G **61**
Bredfield Rd. IP12: Wood 4G **23**
Bredfield St. IP12: Wood 6G **23**
Brendon Dr. IP5: Rus A 3C **38**
Brett Av. IP7: Had 2F **49**
Brett Cl. IP1: Ips 1F **35**
Brettenham Cres. IP4: Ips 6C **28**
Bretts, The IP5: Kes 1H **39**
Breydon Way IP3: Ips 4A **46**
Briardale IP4: Ips 3E **37**
Briarhayes Cl. IP2: Ips 6A **36**
Briarwood Rd. IP12: Wood 2F **33**
Brickfield Cl. IP2: Ips 6B **36** (6E **5**)
Brickfields, The IP14: S'ket 5C **6**
Brick Kiln Cvn. Pk. IP6: N Mar 4B **10**
Brick Kiln Cl. IP11: T Mart 2D **60**
Brick Kiln La. IP9: Hark 6A **58**
IP12: Mel 4D **24**
Brickmakers Ct. IP11: T Mart 1D **60**
Bridewell Wlk. IP12: Wood 6G **23**
Bridge Bus. Cen. IP12: Mart 3D **32**
Bridge Pl. CO11: Catt 6F **55**
Bridge Rd. IP11: Fel 6B **62**
IP12: Brom 2G **25**
Bridge St. IP1: Ips 4B **36** (4D **4**)
IP6: N Mar 3D **10**
IP7: Had .2D **48**
IP14: S'ket 6E **7**
(not continuous)
Bridge Trad. Est. IP6: Gt Bla 4C **16**
Bridge Vw. IP3: Ips 2E **45**
Bridgewood Rd. IP12: Wood 6F **23**
Bridgwater Rd. IP2: Ips 1E **43**
Bridle Way IP1: Ips 1B **36**
Bridport Av. IP3: Ips 6A **38**
Brights Wlk. IP5: Kes 2H **39**

BRIGHTWELL 6C 40
Brightwell Cl. IP11: Fel 1B 64
Brimstone Rd. IP8: Ips 3F 43
Brimwade Cl. CO11: Bran 6G 55
Brinkley Way IP11: Fel 4E 63
Brisbane Rd. IP4: Ips 3A 38
Bristol Hill IP9: S Gate 6H 59
Bristol Hill Pk. IP9: S Gate 6H 59
Bristol Rd. IP4: Ips 2F 37
Britannia Rd. IP4: Ips 3G 37
Britten Av. IP14: S'ket 4C 6
Broadlands Way IP4: Rus A 4C 38
Broad Mdw. IP8: Ips 1D 42
Broadmere Rd. IP1: Ips 1F 35
Broad Oke IP1: Ips 2A 4
Broad Rd. IP13: W Mar 4E 13
Broadwater Gdns. IP9: S Gate 6G 59
Broadway IP13: W Mar 4E 13
Broadway La. IP1: Ips 5F 27
Broadway Vs. *IP1: Ips* *5F 27*
(off Broadway La.)
Brock La. IP12: Mart 3D 32
Brockley Cres. IP1: Ips 6E 27
Broke Av. IP8: Bram 5C 26
BROKE HALL 4C 38
Broke Hall Gdns. IP3: Ips 5A 38
Broke Hall Ho. IP3: Ips 6A 38
BROMESWELL 3F 25
Bromeswell Green Nature Reserve 4E 25
Bromeswell Rd. IP4: Ips 6D 28
Bromley Cl. IP2: Ips 6B 36
Brook Farm La. IP9: Holb 2E 57
Brookfield Rd. IP1: Ips 1G 35
Brookhill Way IP4: Rus A 5C 38
Brookhouse Bus. Pk. IP2: Ips 3G 35
Brooklands Ri. CO11: Bran 5G 55
Brooklands Rd. CO11: Bran 6F 55
Brook La. IP6: Play 3D 30
IP9: Cap 1B 50
IP10: Falk 1G 61
IP11: Fel 6C 62
Brooks Hall Rd. IP1: Ips 2H 35
Brook St. CO7: Ded 6E 53
IP12: Wood 6H 23
Brookview IP8: Ips 2F 43
Broom Cres. IP3: Ips 2E 45
Broom Fld. IP11: Fel 2A 64
Broomfield IP5: Mart H 2A 40
Broomfield Comn. IP8: Spro 3C 34
Broomfield M. IP5: Mart H 2B 40
Broomhayes IP2: Ips 1H 43
Broomheath IP12: Wood 2F 33
BROOM HILL
Ipswich 2C 26
Woodbridge 2E 33
Broom Hill Nature Reserve 4D 48
Broomhill Pool 1H 35
Broom Hill Rd. IP1: Ips 1H 35
Broom Knoll CO7: E Ber 3F 55
Broomspath Rd. IP14: S'and 3G 7
Broomvale Bus. Pk. IP8: L Bla 6B 16
Broom Way IP9: Cap 1E 51
Brotherton Av. IP11: T Mary 3F 61
Broughton Rd. IP1: Ips 2A 36
Browning Rd. CO11: Bran 6F 55
IP1: Ips 4G 27
Brownlow Rd. IP11: Fel 1G 65
Browns Gro. IP5: Kes 2G 39
Brunel Rd. IP2: Ips 3F 35
Brunswick Rd. IP4: Ips 1E 37
Bryon Av. IP11: Fel 2A 64
Buckenham Rd. IP7: Had 5G 49
Buckfast Cl. IP2: Ips 1H 43
Buckingham Cl. IP12: Mart 5B 32
BUCKLESHAM 6H 47
Bucklesham Rd. IP3: Ips 1A 46
IP10: Buc, Fox . . . . . . .2F 47 & 5G 47
Buck's Horns La. IP8: Bel 4C 42
Buddleia Cl. IP2: Ips 5F 35
Bude Cl. IP5: Kes 3D 38
Bugsby Way IP5: Kes 2H 39
Bullard's La. IP12: Wood 6F 23
Bullen Cl. IP8: Bram 5B 26
Bullen La. IP8: Bram 6A 26
(not continuous)

Bull Hall La. IP6: Wit 4G 19
Bull's Cliff IP11: Fel 2E 65
Bull's Rd. IP6: Barh 2F 17
Bulstrode Rd. IP2: Ips 5C 36 (6E 5)
Bulwer Rd. IP1: Ips 2H 35 (1A 4)
Bunting Rd. IP2: Ips 6E 35
Buntings, The IP14: S'ket 6H 7
Bunyan Cl. IP1: Ips 4H 27
Buregate Rd. IP11: Fel 3E 65
Bures Cl. IP14: S'ket 1E 9
Burgess Pl. IP5: Mart H 2C 40
BURGH 2H 21
Burghley Cl. IP2: Ips 1H 43
Burke Cl. IP2: Ips 4H 27
Burke Rd. IP1: Ips 4G 27
Burkitt Ho. IP12: Wood 6H 23
Burkitt Rd. IP12: Wood 6G 23
Burlingham Ho. IP2: Ips 6A 4
Burlington Rd. IP1: Ips 3A 36 (2A 4)
Burnet Cl. IP8: Ips 3E 43
Burnham Cl. IP4: Ips 3E 37
IP11: T Mary 4F 61
Burns Rd. IP1: Ips 4F 27
Burnt Oak CO7: E Ber 4A 54
Burnt Oak Cnr. CO7: E Ber 4A 54
Burrell Rd. IP2: Ips 5A 36 (5B 4)
Burrows Rd. IP12: Mel 1B 24
Burstall La. IP8: Spro 3A 34
Burton Dr. IP6: N Mar 3C 10
Burwash IP6: Wit 3F 19
Burwood Pl. IP11: T Mary 3F 61
Bury Hill IP12: Wood 4H 23
Bury Hill Cl. IP12: Wood 4H 23
Bury Rd. IP1: Ips 3E 27
IP14: S'ket 1A 6
(Fishponds Way)
IP14: S'ket 3D 6
(Gipping Pl.)
Bury St. IP14: S'ket 5D 6
Bushey Cl. IP9: Cap 2D 50
Bushman Gdns. IP8: Bram 5B 26
Butchers La. IP9: Cap 2E 51
Butler Smith Gdns. IP5: Kes 2F 39
Butley Cl. IP2: Ips 3G 43
Butley Rd. IP11: Fel 2D 64
Buttercup Cl. IP8: Ips 2D 42
Butterfly Gdns. IP4: Rus A 4B 38
Butter Mkt. IP1: Ips 3B 36 (2D 4)
IP14: S'ket *5D 6*
(off Market Pl.)
Buttermarket Shop. Cen.
IP1: Ips 3B 36 (2D 4)
Buttermere Grn. IP11: Fel 5E 63
Buttrum's Tower Mill 6F 23
Bylam La. IP9: Chel 3A 58
Byland Cl. IP2: Ips 1H 43
Byles Wlk. IP14: S'ket 5C 6
Byng Hall Rd. IP13: Pett, Uff 3C 14
Byng La. IP13: Pett 3B 14
Byron Rd. IP1: Ips 3F 27

C

Cadmus Rd. IP1: Ips 2E 35
Cage La. IP11: Fel 6H 61
Cages Way IP12: Mel 1B 24
Caithness Cl. IP4: Ips 1G 37
Calais St. IP7: Had 3E 49
Calder Rd. IP2: Ips 1B 44
Caledonia Rd. IP9: S Gate 6H 59
CALIFORNIA 3F 37
. . . . .6C 12
California IP12: Wood 2E 33
Camberley Rd. IP4: Ips 2A 38
Camborne Rd. IP5: Kes 2E 39
Cambridge Dr. IP2: Ips 2F 43
Cambridge Rd. IP5: Kes 1D 38
IP11: Fel 1G 65
Camden Rd. IP1: Ips 5G 37
Campbell Rd. IP3: Ips 1H 45
Campion Cres. IP14: S'ket 1C 8
Campion Rd. IP2: Ips 5G 35
Camwood Gdns. IP3: Ips 5G 37
Canberra Cl. IP4: Ips 3A 38
Candlet Gro. IP11: Fel 6A 62

Candlet Rd. IP11: Fel 4H 61
Canham St. IP1: Ips 3A 36 (2B 4)
Canterbury Cl. IP2: Ips 3G 43
Canterbury Gdns. IP7: Had 3F 49
Capel Cl. IP11: T Mart 1E 61
Capel Dr. IP11: Fel 1B 64
Capel Hall La. IP11: T Mart 1F 61
Capel Rd. IP9: B'ley 4F 51
Capelgrove IP9: Cap 3C 50
CAPEL ST MARY 2D 50
CAPEL ST MARY INTERCHANGE 2F 51
Carders Cl. IP7: Had 5E 49
Cardew Drift IP5: Kes 1G 39
Cardiff Av. IP2: Ips 2A 44
Cardigan St. IP1: Ips 2A 36
Cardinalls Rd. IP14: S'ket 4D 6
Cardinal Pk. E. IP1: Ips 4C 4
Cardinal Pk. W. IP1: Ips 4B 4
Cardinals Ct. IP11: Fel 2F 65
Cardinal St. IP1: Ips 4B 36 (4C 4)
Carlford Cl. IP5: Mart H 1B 40
Carlford Ct. IP4: Ips 4G 37
Carlow M. IP12: Wood 6H 23
Carlton Rd. IP5: Kes 2D 38
Carlton Wlk. IP7: Had 5F 49
Carlton Way IP4: Ips 1D 36
Carlyle Cl. IP1: Ips 3G 27
Carmarthen Cl. IP2: Ips 2H 43
Carmelite Pl. IP12: Wood 1H 33
Carol Av. IP12: Mart 6B 32
Carolbrook Rd. IP2: Ips 4F 43
Carol Cl. IP11: Fel 6D 62
Carriage Cl. IP11: T Mary 3F 61
Carriers Ct. CO7: E Ber 2A 54
Carr Rd. IP11: Fel 5C 64
Carr St. IP4: Ips 3C 36 (2E 5)
Carthew Ct. IP12: Wood 1H 33
Case La. IP9: B'ley 4G 51
Castle Cl. IP11: Fel 5E 63
Castle Ct. IP11: Fel 4H 27
CASTLE HILL 4A 28
Castle Hill IP12: Eyk 1H 25
Castle La. IP7: Had 2D 48
Castle Ri. IP7: Had 2D 48
Castle Rd. IP1: Ips 6F 27
IP7: Had 2C 48
Castle St. IP12: Wood 6H 23
Catchpole Dr. IP5: Kes 3F 39
Catchpoles Way IP3: Ips 3E 45
Catesbray IP9: Cap 2C 50
Catherine Rd. IP12: Wood 6F 23
CATTAWADE 6F 55
Cattawade St. CO11: Catt 6F 55
Catts Cl. IP9: Sutt 6B 56
Cattsfield IP9: Sutt 6B 56
Cauldwell Av. IP4: Ips 3E 37
Cauldwell Hall Rd. IP4: Ips 3E 37
Causeway, The IP6: N Mar 4C 10
Cavan Rd. IP1: Ips 5E 27
Cavendish Gdns. IP11: T Mart 1E 61
Cavendish Rd. IP11: Fel 2E 65
IP11: T Mart 1D 60
IP14: S'ket 5B 6
Cavendish St. IP3: Ips 5D 36 (5H 5)
Cecilia St. IP1: Ips 4B 36 (4C 4)
Cecil Rd. IP1: Ips 3A 36 (1B 4)
Cedar Av. IP5: Kes 3D 38
Cedar Cl. CO11: Bran 4G 55
Cedarcroft Rd. IP1: Ips 5G 27
Cedar Ho. IP2: Ips 6H 35
Cedars La. IP9: Cap 2C 50
Cedars Link Rd. IP14: S'ket 6G 7
Cemetery La. CO7: E Ber 3G 53
IP4: Ips 1D 36
IP12: Wood 1F 33
Cemetery Rd. IP4: Ips 3C 36 (1F 5)
Centenary Ho. IP11: Fel 2A 64
Central Av. IP3: Ips 3A 46
Central Maltings *IP12: Wood* *1H 33*
(off Crown Pl.)
Central Rd. IP11: Fel 2A 64
Centre, The IP2: Ips 2H 43
Century Dr. IP5: Kes 2G 39
Cerdic Ho. IP11: Fel 5B 64
Chainhouse Rd. IP6: N Mar 4D 10
Chalfont Sq. IP4 . . . . .2E 5

Chalkeith Rd. IP6: N Mar	..........5E 11	
Chalk Hill La. IP6: Gt Bla	.........3A 16	
Chalkners Cl. IP9: Cap	.............2D 50	
Chalon St. IP1: Ips	.......4A 36 (4B 4)	
Chamberlain Way IP8: Ips	.........1C 42	
Chancery Rd. IP1: Ips	.......4A 36 (4A 4)	
Chandlers Wlk. IP14: S'ket	........1D 8	
Chandos Ct. IP12: Mart	...........5B 32	
Chandos Dr. IP12: Mart	...........5B 32	
CHANTRY	...............5F 35	
Chantry Cl. IP2: Ips	...........5F 35	
Chantry Grn. IP2: Ips	...........6E 35	
Chantry High Sports Cen.	...........6G 35	
Chantry Home Cvn. Pk. IP2: Ips	...4F 35	
Chapel Cl. IP9: Cap	............2D 50	
Chapel Fld. IP8: Bram	...........5B 26	
Chapel La. IP6: Gt Bla	...........5B 16	
IP8: Bel	...............4D 42	
IP8: Wash	.............2B 42	
IP13: Grun	.............4G 21	
IP13: Pett, W Mar	........5F 13	
IP14: S'and	.............3H 7	
Chapel M. IP4: Ips	...............1E 5	
Chapel Rd. IP13: Grun	...........4G 21	
Chapel St. IP12: Wood	...........6H 23	
Chaplin Rd. CO7: E Ber	..........2H 53	
Charles Av. IP13: Grun	...........3F 21	
Charles Ind. Est., The IP14: S'ket	...4E 7	
Charles Rd. IP11: Fel	............2D 64	
Charles St. IP1: Ips	.......3B 36 (1C 4)	
Charlotte's IP8: Wash	...........2A 42	
Charlton Av. IP1: Ips	............5G 27	
Charter Cl. IP7: Had	............2E 49	
Chartwell Cl. IP4: Ips	...........4F 37	
Chase, The CO11: Bran	..........4H 55	
IP5: Mart H	............2B 40	
IP11: Fel	..............1E 65	
Chaser Cl. IP3: Ips	.............3H 45	
Chatsworth Cres. IP2: Ips	.......1H 43	
IP11: T Mary	..........4F 61	
Chatsworth Dr. IP4: Rus A	.......4B 38	
Chattisham Cl. IP14: S'ket	.......2E 9	
Chaucer Rd. IP1: Ips	............4G 27	
IP11: Fel	..............2E 65	
CHELMONDISTON	...........3C 58	
Chelsea Cl. IP1: Ips	.............6G 27	
Chelsworth Av. IP1: Ips	..........6C 28	
Chelsworth Rd. IP11: Fel	.........1C 64	
Chelsworth Way IP14: S'ket	......2E 9	
Cheltenham Av. IP1: Ips	.........6A 28	
Chepstow Rd. IP1: Ips	...........3A 28	
IP11: Fel	..............6A 62	
Chequers Ri. IP6: Gt Bla	.........1C 42	
Cherry Blossom Cl. IP8: Ips	......1C 42	
Cherry Flds. IP8: Bram	..........6B 26	
Cherry La. IP4: Ips	.............2G 37	
Cherry La. Gdns. IP4: Ips	........2G 37	
Cherry Tree Rd. IP12: Wood	......1G 33	
IP14: S'ket	.............4C 6	
Chesapeake Cl. IP9: Chel	.........3C 58	
Chesapeake Rd. IP3: Ips	.........3F 45	
Chesham Rd. IP2: Ips	.....5A 36 (6B 4)	
Chessington Gdns. IP1: Ips	.......1G 35	
Chesterfield Dr. IP1: Ips	.........5G 27	
Chester Rd. IP11: Fel	...........1A 64	
Chesterton Cl. IP2: Ips	..........1F 43	
Chestnut Cl. IP5: Rus A	..........6B 30	
IP14: S'and	.............3G 7	
Chestnut Dr. IP6: Cla	............5D 16	
Chestnut Gro. IP14: S'ket	........1E 5	
Chestnuts, The IP2: Ips	..........1D 42	
Chevalier Rd. IP11: Fel	..........1G 65	
Chevallier St. IP1: Ips	...........2H 35	
Childer Rd. IP14: S'ket	...........5D 6	
Childers Fld. IP11: Fel	...........6G 61	
Chiltern Ct. IP2: Ips	............6A 36	
Chilton Av. IP14: S'ket	...........5C 6	
Chilton Ct. IP14: S'ket	...........5C 6	
Chilton Rd. IP3: Ips	.............4H 37	
Chilton Way IP14: S'ket	..........4A 6	
Chisnall Cl. IP7: Had	............1E 49	
Christchurch Ct. IP4: Ips	.........1E 5	
Christchurch Dr. IP12: Wood	......2E 33	
Christchurch Mansion & Wolsey Gallery		
	...............1E 5	
Christchurch St. IP4: Ips	...2C 36 (1F 5)	

Church Cl. IP5: Kes	............1E 39	
IP8: Spro	..............3B 34	
IP10: Buc	.............5H 47	
Church Cres. IP8: Spro	..........3B 34	
CHURCH END	.............2F 59	
Church Fld. IP6: Gt Bla	..........3A 16	
Church Fld. Rd. IP9: Sutt	.........6C 56	
Church Grn. IP8: Bram	..........6C 26	
Church Hill IP9: Holb	...........4F 57	
Churchill Av. IP4: Ips	...........4F 37	
IP7: Had	..............2E 49	
Churchill Cl. IP12: Wood	.........1F 33	
Churchill Cres. IP13: W Mar	......4F 13	
Church La. CO11: Bran	..........4H 55	
IP6: C Mary	............1E 11	
IP6: Cla	...............5D 16	
IP6: Hen	..............2B 18	
IP6: Play	..............3E 31	
IP6: West	.............3E 29	
IP6: Wit	...............3E 19	
IP8: Spro	..............3C 34	
(not continuous)		
IP9: Chel	.............2A 58	
IP10: Buc	.............5H 47	
IP11: Fel	..............5H 61	
IP11: T Mart	...........2E 61	
IP12: Brom	............3F 25	
IP12: Eyk	.............1H 25	
IP12: Mart	............5E 33	
IP13: Uff	..............6E 15	
IP14: S'ket	.............5D 6	
Churchman Cl. IP12: Mel	.........3A 24	
Church Mdws. IP6: Hen	..........2A 18	
Church Rd. IP6: Play	............3E 31	
IP9: B'ley	.............5H 51	
IP9: Sutt	..............6C 56	
IP9: Tatt	..............1A 56	
IP11: Fel	..............5D 62	
IP13: Has	.............4C 22	
IP14: Comb, S'ket	........2D 8	
IP14: S'and	.............3H 7	
Church St. IP7: Had	............4E 49	
IP9: Chel	.............3B 58	
IP12: Wood	............6H 23	
Church Ter. IP13: W Mar	.........5F 13	
Church Vw. Cl. IP12: Mel	........4B 24	
Church Wlk. IP7: Had	...........3E 49	
IP14: S'ket	.............5D 6	
(off Church La.)		
Cinnabar Cl. IP8: Ips	...........3F 43	
Civic Dr. IP1: Ips	.......3A 36 (2B 4)	
Claire Cl. IP14: S'ket	...........2E 9	
Clapgate La. IP3: Ips	...........6F 37	
Clappers Path IP13: Uff	..........5D 14	
Clare Av. IP12: Wood	...........1F 33	
Clarence Rd. IP3: Ips	...........2G 45	
Clarendon Rd. IP4: Ips	..........1E 37	
Clarice House Leisure Cen.	.........6D 26	
Clarkson St. IP1: Ips	......3H 35 (1A 4)	
Claude St. IP1: Ips	.......3B 36 (1C 4)	
Claverton Way IP4: Rus A	........4A 38	
CLAYDON	...............5D 16	
Claydon Ind. Pk. IP6: Gt Bla	......4B 16	
Clayton Cl. IP12: Wood	..........2E 33	
Clearwing Cl. IP8: Ips	...........3F 43	
Clementine Gdns. IP4: Ips	........4F 37	
Clements Rd. IP12: Mel	..........4B 24	
Clench Cl. IP4: Ips	......3C 36 (2F 5)	
Clench Rd. IP9: Holb	...........1F 57	
Cliff Ct. IP11: Fel	.............5E 63	
Cliff La. IP3: Ips	..............6D 36	
Clifford Rd. IP4: Ips	............6E 37	
Cliff Rd. IP3: Ips	.........6D 36 (6G 5)	
IP11: Fel	..............6E 63	
Clifton Way IP2: Ips	............1E 43	
Clifton Wood IP9: Holb	..........2F 57	
Clive Av. IP1: Ips	.............5A 28	
Cloncurry Gdns. IP11: Fel	........2C 64	
Clopton Gdns. IP7: Had	.........4E 49	
Clopton Rd. IP6: Grun, Swil, Tudd	..6H 19	
IP13: Grun	.............3A 20	
Close, The IP9: Tatt	............1A 56	
Clovelly Cl. IP4: Rus A	..........5C 38	
Clover Cl. IP2: Ips	.............5G 35	
IP6: N Mar	.............5D 10	
Clovers Ct. IP14: S'ket	..........5C 6	

Clump Fld. IP2: Ips	.............1G 43	
Coachmans Ct. IP4: Ips	..........3D 4	
Coachmans Paddock IP9: Holb	.....2F 57	
Cobbold M. IP4: Ips	........3C 36 (1F 5)	
Cobbold Rd. IP11: Fel	...........1F 65	
IP12: Wood	............4F 23	
Cobbold St. IP4: Ips	......3C 36 (1E 5)	
Cobden Pl. IP4: Ips	......3C 36 (2E 5)	
Cobham Rd. IP3: Ips	...........6H 37	
Cockfield Hall La. IP6: West, Wit	...6D 18	
Coddenham Rd. IP6: C Mary, N Mar	..4E 11	
(not continuous)		
Cody Rd. IP3: Ips	.............2H 45	
Colbourne Ct. IP11: Fel	..........1F 65	
(off Ranelagh Rd.)		
Colchester Rd. IP4: Ips	..........6E 29	
Cold Store Rd. IP11: Fel	.........4B 64	
Cole Ness Rd. IP3: Ips	..........3F 45	
Coleridge Rd. IP1: Ips	..........4G 27	
Coles Oak La. CO7: Ded	.........6A 52	
College Grn. IP11: Fel	...........6D 62	
College St. IP4: Ips	......4B 36 (4D 4)	
Collett's Wlk. IP12: Wood	........6E 23	
(not continuous)		
Collimer Cl. IP9: Chel	...........2B 58	
Collimer Ct. IP11: Fel	...........5H 61	
Collingwood Av. IP3: Ips	.........1G 45	
Collingwood Flds. CO7: E Ber	......1G 53	
Collingwood Rd. IP12: Wood	......4G 23	
Collinson's IP2: Ips	............4E 35	
Colneis Rd. IP11: Fel	...........5B 62	
Coltsfoot Rd. IP2: Ips	...........5F 35	
Columbia Cl. IP5: Kes	...........2D 38	
Columbine Gdns. IP2: Ips	........4F 35	
Columbyne Cl. IP14: S'and	.......2H 7	
Combers, The IP5: Kes	..........2H 39	
COMBS	................3C 8	
Combs Ct. IP14: S'ket	...........1D 8	
COMBS FORD	...............1E 9	
Combs Grn. IP14: Comb	.........5A 8	
Combs La. IP14: Gt Fin, S'ket	......6A 6	
Combs Wood Dr. IP14: S'ket	......2D 8	
Combs Wood Nature Reserve	.......3E 9	
Commercial Rd. IP1: Ips	....5A 36 (5B 4)	
COMMON, THE	.............1A 26	
Common La. IP12: Brom	.........4E 25	
Conach Rd. IP12: Wood	..........6F 23	
Congreve Rd. IP1: Ips	...........4H 27	
Coniston Cl. IP11: Fel	...........4F 63	
Coniston Rd. IP3: Ips	...........1G 45	
Coniston Sq. E. IP3: Ips	..........1G 45	
Coniston Sq. W. IP3: Ips	.........1G 45	
Connaught Rd. IP1: Ips	..........5E 27	
Constable M. CO7: Ded	..........6E 53	
IP11: Fel	..............1G 65	
Constable Rd. IP4: Ips	...........2C 36	
Constable Row CO7: Ded	.........6F 53	
Constable Wlk. IP14: S'ket	.......4C 6	
Constantine Rd. IP1: Ips	....4A 36 (4A 4)	
Constitution Hill IP1: Ips	.........1A 36	
IP6: N Mar	.............3D 10	
Convalescent Hill IP11: Fel	........2F 65	
Conway Cl. IP1: Ips	............1A 44	
IP11: Fel	..............4D 62	
Cooks Cl. IP5: Kes	.............1H 39	
Cooks Hill IP13: Leth	...........1A 12	
Coombers IP9: Cap	............2C 50	
Coopers Cl. IP6: Wit	............1F 19	
Coopers Rd. IP5: Mart H	.........2C 40	
IP6: Barh	..............2F 17	
Coopers Way IP6: Barh	..........4C 16	
COPDOCK	...............4A 42	
COPDOCK MILL INTERCHANGE	........3C 42	
Copleston Cen.	..............4H 37	
Copleston Rd. IP4: Ips	..........4G 37	
Copperfield Rd. IP2: Ips	..........4F 35	
Copper Gro. IP8: Ips	...........3F 43	
(off Ellenbrook Rd.)		
IP8: Ips	...............3F 43	
(Marbled White Dr.)		
Coppice Cl. IP12: Mel	...........5H 23	
Coprolite St. IP3: Ips	.......5D 36 (4G 5)	
Copswood Cl. IP5: Kes	..........2A 40	
Coral Dr. IP1: Ips	.............6E 27	
Coram St. IP7: Had	............5A 48	
Corder Rd. IP4: Ips	............1C 36	

Cordwinders CO7: E Ber 4B 54
Cordy's La. IP11: T Mary 5E 61
Cork Pl. IP1: Ips 5E 27
Corks La. IP7: Had 3D 48
Corn Exchange 2C 4
Cornflower Cl. IP2: Ips 5F 35
Cornhill IP1: Ips 2C 4
Cornwallis Ter. IP4: Ips 3E 37
Cornwall Rd. IP11: Fel 6H 61
Coronation Dr. IP11: Fel 2C 64
Coronation Rd. IP4: Ips 4G 37
Corporation Av. IP2: Ips 3H 43
Corton Rd. IP3: Ips 2G 45
Cotman Rd. IP3: Ips 2F 45
Cotswold Av. IP1: Ips 6A 28
Cottage Pl. IP1: Ips 1B 4
Cottesford Cl. IP7: Had 4F 49
Cottingham Rd. IP8: Ips 1C 42
Courts, The IP6: Play 2E 31
      IP11: Fel 1G 65
Courtyard, The IP14: S'ket 4B 6
Cowell St. IP2: Ips 6B 36
Cow La. IP9: S'ly 2E 59
Cowley Rd. IP11: Fel 1F 65
Cowper St. IP4: Ips 3G 37
Cowslip Cl. IP2: Ips 5G 35
Cowslip Way IP6: N Mar 5D 10
Cox Cl. IP5: Kes 3E 39
Cox La. IP4: Ips 3C 36 (2E 5)
                        (not continuous)
Coytes Gdns. IP1: Ips 4B 36 (3C 4)
Crabbe St. IP4: Ips 3F 37
Craig Cl. IP11: T Mart 1E 61
Cranborne Chase IP4: Ips 6F 29
                  (off Wincanton Cl.)
Cranbourne Cl. IP4: Ips 6F 29
Crane Cl. IP12: Wood 2E 33
Crane Hill IP2: Ips 4F 35
Cranfield Ct. IP4: Ips 6D 28
Cranmer Cliff Gdns. IP11: Fel 6E 63
Cranwell Cres. IP3: Ips 2H 45
Cranwell Gro. IP5: Kes 2F 39
Cranworth Cl. IP13: Grun 2F 21
Cranworth Rd. IP7: Had 5F 49
Crawford La. IP5: Kes 2F 39
Creeting Rd. IP14: S'ket, S'and ...5E 7
Crepping Hall Dr. IP9: Sutt 6A 56
Crescent, The IP6: Barh 2B 16
      IP13: W Mar 5E 13
      IP14: S'ket 1E 9
Crescent Rd. IP1: Ips 3A 36 (1A 4)
      IP11: Fel 1F 65
Cricket Hill Rd. IP11: Fel 6G 61
Crockatt Rd. IP7: Had 1F 49
Crocus Cl. IP2: Ips 5G 35
Crofton Cl. IP4: Ips 2G 37
Crofton Rd. IP4: Ips 2G 37
Croft St. IP2: Ips 6B 36
Cromarty Rd. IP4: Ips 1G 37
Cromer Rd. IP1: Ips 1G 35
Crompton Rd. IP2: Ips 2G 35
Cromwell Cl. IP1: Ips 4B 36 (4C 4)
Cromwell Sq. IP1: Ips 4B 36 (3C 4)
Crossgate Fld. IP11: Fel 6H 61
Crossley Gdns. IP11: Fel 5D 26
Cross Maltings IP7: Had 4E 49
Cross St. IP11: Fel 5H 61
Crotchets Cl. IP9: Cap 1D 50
Croutel Rd. IP11: Fel 6C 62
Crowe St. IP14: S'ket 5D 6
Crow Hall La. IP9: Sutt 6C 56
Crowland Cl. IP2: Ips 1H 43
Crow La. IP14: S'ket 6D 6
Crowley Rd. IP6: N Mar 4D 10
Crown Cl. IP12: Mart 5C 32
Crownfields IP13: Uff 5D 14
Crown Ho. IP1: Ips 3B 36 (1C 4)
Crown La. IP13: W Mar 5F 13
Crown Pl. IP12: Wood 1H 33
Crown Pools Swimming Complex 1D 4
Crown St. CO7: Ded 6E 53
      IP1: Ips 3B 36 (1C 4)
      IP6: N Mar 3D 10
      IP11: Fel 6H 61
      IP14: S'ket 4D 6
Crowswell Cl. IP11: T Mart 1E 61

Cuckfield Av. IP3: Ips 6B 38
Culford Pl. IP3: Ips 5E 37
Culford Wlk. IP11: Fel 2B 64
Cullingham Rd. IP1: Ips 3H 35
CULPHO 6C 20
Cumberland Cl. IP11: Fel 5E 63
Cumberland M. IP12: Wood 1H 33
Cumberland St. IP1: Ips 2A 36
      IP12: Wood 1G 33
Cumberland Twr. IP1: Ips 2H 35
                     (off Norwich Rd.)
Curlew Rd. IP2: Ips 6E 35
Curriers La. IP1: Ips 4B 36 (2C 4)
Curtis Cl. IP8: Ips 2D 42
Curtis Way IP5: Kes 3G 39
Curwen Rd. IP14: S'ket 5C 6
Cutlers La. CO7: Stra M, E Ber 5A 50
Cutler St. IP1: Ips 4B 36 (4C 4)

D

Daffodil Cl. IP2: Ips 6F 35
Daimler Rd. IP1: Ips 5D 26
Daines La. IP12: Mel 4B 24
Dains Pl. IP11: T Mary 4F 61
Dale Hall La. IP1: Ips 5A 28
Dales Rd. IP1: Ips 6G 27
Dales Vw. Rd. IP1: Ips 1H 35
Dallinghoo Rd. IP13: W Mar 6B 12
Dalton Rd. IP1: Ips 3A 36 (2A 4)
Damselfly Rd. IP3: Ips 3H 45
Dandalan Cl. IP1: Ips 1F 35
Danes Cl. IP14: S'ket 6C 6
Danescourt Av. IP14: S'ket 6C 6
Dangerous La. IP6: Barh 1D 16
Darrell Rd. IP11: Fel 4C 64
Darsham Cl. IP11: Fel 1C 64
Darter Cl. IP3: Ips 3H 45
Darwin Rd. IP4: Ips 4E 37
Dashwood Cl. IP8: Ips 2E 43
Daundy Cl. IP2: Ips 4E 35
Davey Cl. IP3: Ips 2E 45
Dawes Cl. IP9: Cap 1C 50
Dawnbrook Cl. IP2: Ips 2F 43
Dawson Drift IP5: Kes 2F 39
Dawson Dr. IP11: T Mary 3F 61
Days Grn. IP9: Cap 2B 50
Days Rd. IP9: Cap 1C 50
Dazeley's La. CO7: E Ber 4C 54
Deacon Ct. IP11: Fel 5E 63
Dead La. CO7: Stra M, E Ber 1F 53
Deben Av. IP5: Mart H 6A 32
Deben Ct. IP13: W Mar 5F 13
Deben Rd. IP1: Ips 6G 27
      IP12: Wood 6A 24
Debenside, The IP12: Mel 4B 24
Deben Swimming Pool 1H 33
Deben Valley Dr. IP5: Kes 2F 39
Deben Vw. IP12: Wood 1H 33
Deben Way IP11: Fel 2D 64
      IP12: Mel 4B 24
De Brink on the Grn. IP5: Mart H ...2B 40
                     (off Jackson Ct.)
DEDHAM 6E 53
Dedham Art & Craft Cen. & Toy Mus. ...6E 53
Dedham Mill CO7: Ded 6E 53
Dedham Pl. IP4: Ips 3E 5
Dedham Rd. CO7: Stra M, Ded 3D 52
Dedham Vale Family Farm 6E 53
Defoe Rd. IP1: Ips 3G 27
Delf Cl. IP7: Had 2F 49
Delius Cl. IP14: S'ket 4C 6
Dellwood Av. IP11: Fel 6B 62
Demesne Gdns. IP5: Mart H 1B 40
Demoiselle Cres. IP3: Ips 3H 45
Denham Ct. IP5: Mart H 3B 40
Denmark Gdns. IP9: Holb 2F 57
Denton Cl. IP2: Ips 1E 43
Derby Cl. IP4: Ips 4F 37
Derby Rd. IP3: Ips 5F 37
Derby Road Station (Rail) 5F 37
Dereham Av. IP3: Ips 6E 37
Derwent Rd. IP3: Ips 6E 37
Deveraux Ct. IP4: Ips 1E 5
Devlin Rd. IP8: Ips 2C 42

Devon Rd. IP11: Fel 6A 62
      IP14: S'and 3G 7
Devonshire Rd. IP3: Ips 4E 37 (4H 5)
Dewar La. IP5: Kes 2F 39
Dhobi Pl. IP1: Ips 2G 35
Dial La. IP1: Ips 3B 36 (2D 4)
Diamond Cl. IP1: Ips 6E 27
Dickens Rd. IP2: Ips 3F 35
Dickinson Ter. IP5: Kes 2G 39
Didsbury Cl. IP2: Ips 1E 43
Digby Cl. IP5: Mart H 3B 40
Digby Rd. IP4: Ips 2H 37
Dillwyn St. IP1: Ips 3H 35 (2A 4)
Dillwyn St. W. IP1: Ips 3H 35 (2A 4)
Dinsdale Ct. IP11: Fel 2E 65
Ditchingham Gro. IP5: Rus A 3C 38
Dobbs Drift IP5: Kes 2A 40
Dobbs La. IP5: Kes 1A 40
      IP10: Fox 4H 39
Dock La. IP12: Mel 4B 24
Dock Rd. IP11: Fel 5C 64
Dock St. IP2: Ips 5B 36 (5D 4)
Doctor Watson's La. IP5: Kes 6D 30
Dodmans IP9: Cap 2D 50
Dodson Va. IP5: Kes 2F 39
Dogs Head St. IP4: Ips 4B 36 (3D 4)
Dogwood Cl. IP3: Pur F 1A 46
Dombey Rd. IP2: Ips 4F 35
Donegal Rd. IP1: Ips 5E 27
Donkey La. CO7: Stra M 4E 53
      IP6: Tudd 2A 30
Dooley Rd. IP11: Fel 2B 64
Dorchester Rd. IP3: Ips 6A 38
Doric Pl. IP12: Wood 1H 33
Dorset Cl. IP4: Ips 6E 29
Dovedale IP11: Fel 2C 64
Dove Gdns. IP14: S'ket 5G 7
Dover Rd. IP3: Ips 5G 37
Dove St. IP4: Ips 4D 36 (3G 5)
Downham Blvd. IP3: Ips 4H 45
Downing Cl. IP2: Ips 1G 43
      IP12: Wood 1F 33
Downs, The IP11: Fel 6G 61
Downside IP14: S'ket 5B 6
Downside Cl. IP2: Ips 3G 43
Dragonfly Wlk. IP3: Ips 3H 45
                  (off Avensworth Av.)
Drake Av. IP3: Ips 1G 45
Drake Cl. IP14: S'ket 5B 6
Drake Sq. Nth. IP3: Ips 1G 45
Drake Sq. Sth. IP3: Ips 1G 45
Drapers Cl. IP7: Had 3F 49
Draymans Way IP3: Ips 6D 36
Drift, The CO7: Ded 6E 53
      CO7: E Ber 3F 55
      IP3: Ips 3F 37
      IP4: Ips 3F 37
      IP5: Mart H 2B 40
      IP6: Hen 2A 18
      IP6: N Mar 5C 10
      IP9: Sutt 6E 57
      IP13: W Mar 4G 13
Drift Ct. IP6: N Mar 4D 10
Driftway, The IP4: Ips 3G 37
      IP13: Grun 1E 23
Drive, The IP5: Mart H 1D 40
Drovers Cl. IP11: T Mary 3E 61
Drum Fld. CO7: Stra M 4C 52
Drury Rd. IP6: Cla 5D 16
DRYBRIDGE HILL 6F 23
Drybridge Hill IP12: Wood 6F 23
Dryden Rd. IP1: Ips 4H 27
Duckamere IP8: Bram 6B 26
Dukes Cl. IP11: Fel 5E 63
Dukes Mdw. IP12: Wood 2E 33
Dukes Pk. IP12: Wood 3E 33
Duke St. IP3: Ips 5D 36 (5G 5)
      IP7: Had 3F 49
Dumbarton Rd. IP4: Ips 1G 37
Dumfries Rd. IP4: Ips 6H 29
Dundee Ho. IP4: Ips 1G 37
Dunlin Rd. IP2: Ips 1F 43
Dunlop Rd. IP2: Ips 3G 35
Dunn Cl. IP7: Had 4F 49
Dunnock Cl. IP14: S'ket 6G 7
Dunton Gro. IP7: Had 5F 49

Dunwich Ct. IP1: Ips 1F 35
Durrant Rd. IP7: Had 2E 49
Durrant Vw. IP5: Kes 2H 39
Dyer Ct. IP7: Had 4G 49
Dyke Rd. IP11: Fel 3A 64
Dykes St. IP1: Ips 2B 36 (1C 4)

E

Eagles Cl. IP11: Fel 1E 65
Eagle St. IP4: Ips 4C 36 (3E 5)
Eagle Way IP5: Mart H 3B 40
Earls Cl. IP11: Fel 5E 63
Easst Row IP9: Holb 2F 57
EAST BERGHOLT 2H 53
East Bergholt Place Gardens 4C 54
East Bergholt Sports Cen. 1A 54
Eastcliff IP11: Fel 4F 63
EAST END 3F 55
East End La. CO7: E Ber 3F 55
East End Rd. CO7: E Ber 3C 54
Eastern Cl. IP4: Rus A 5C 38
Eastgate Shop. Cen. IP4: Ips ...3C 36 (2E 5)
Eastland Ct. IP11: T Mary 4G 61
East La. IP13: Uff 5F 15
East Lawn IP4: Ips 1H 37
Easton Rd. IP13: Hach 3E 13
East Vw. Terraces IP9: S Gate 5G 59
Eastward Pl. IP14: S'ket 4C 6
Eastway Ent. Cen. IP1: Ips 1E 35
Eaton Cl. IP11: T Mary 4F 61
Eaton Gdns. IP11: Fel 3D 64
Eccles Rd. IP2: Ips 1E 43
Eddowes Rd. IP6: Barh 4D 16
Eden Rd. IP4: Ips 4G 37
Edgar Av. IP14: S'ket 1D 8
Edgecomb Rd. IP14: S'ket 2D 8
Edgeworth Rd. IP2: Ips 1F 43
Edinburgh Cl. IP14: S'ket 5E 7
Edinburgh Gdns. IP6: Cla 4D 16
Edmonton Cl. IP5: Kes 2D 38
Edmonton Rd. IP5: Kes 1D 38
Edward Cl. IP1: Ips 1G 35
Edward Fitzgerald Ct. IP12: Wood 5F 23
Edwin Av. IP12: Wood 4G 23
Edwin Panks Rd. IP7: Had 3F 49
Edwin Ter. IP12: Wood 5G 23
Egglestone Cl. IP2: Ips 2G 43
Eldred Cl. IP1: Ips 1E 35
Eliot Way IP14: S'ket 3B 6
Elizabeth Cl. IP3: Ips 4H 5
Elizabeth Way IP11: Fel 2C 64
    IP14: S'ket 5E 7
Ellenbrook Grn. IP2: Ips 2E 43
Ellenbrook Rd. IP2: Ips 2E 43
    IP8: Ips 2E 43
Elliott St. IP1: Ips 3H 35 (2A 4)
Elm Cl. CO11: Bran 4G 55
Elm Ct. IP1: Ips 2C 4
Elmcroft La. IP11: Fel 4D 62
    (not continuous)
Elmcroft Rd. IP1: Ips 5H 27
Elmers La. IP5: Kes 2G 39
Elm Est. CO7: E Ber 2H 53
Elm Gdns. IP11: T Mary 4F 61
Elmham Dr. IP10: Nac 3E 47
Elm Ho. IP11: Fel 6H 61
Elmhurst Cl. IP12: Wood 6A 24
Elmhurst Dr. IP3: Ips 6E 37
Elmhurst Wlk. IP12: Wood 6A 24
Elm La. IP8: Cop 3A 42
    IP9: Cap 2D 50
Elm Rd. CO7: E Ber 2G 53
    IP5: Rus A 2C 38
    IP13: W Mar 5E 13
    IP14: S'ket 5C 6
Elmsett Cl. IP14: S'ket 2F 9
Elm St. IP1: Ips 3A 36 (2B 4)
Elsmere Rd. IP1: Ips 1B 36
Elton Bus. Cen. IP2: Ips 3F 35
Elton Pk. IP2: Ips 3E 35
Elton Pk. Ind. Est. IP2: Ips 3F 35
Ely Rd. IP4: Ips 6E 29
    IP6: Barh, Cla 4E 17
Emerald Cl. IP5: Kes 1F 39

Emerson Way IP7: Had 2E 49
Emily Bray Ho. IP4: Ips 1H 5
Emlen St. IP1: Ips 3H 35 (2A 4)
Emmanuel Cl. IP2: Ips 1G 43
Emperor Cir. IP3: Ips 3H 45
Ennerdale Cl. IP11: Fel 5E 63
Epsom Dr. IP1: Ips 3H 27
Ernleigh Rd. IP4: Ips 3G 37
Essex Way IP3: Pur F 2B 46
Estuary Cres. IP9: S Gate 6H 59
Estuary Dr. IP11: Fel 4E 63
Estuary Rd. IP9: S Gate 6G 59
Europa Way IP1: Ips 1D 34
Eustace Rd. IP1: Ips 1F 35
Euston Av. IP4: Rus A 3C 38
Euston Ct. IP11: Fel 1B 64
Evabrook Cl. IP2: Ips 2F 43
Everton Cres. IP1: Ips 6G 27
Evesham Cl. IP2: Ips 1H 43
Exeter Rd. IP3: Ips 5G 37
    IP6: Cla 4E 17
    IP11: Fel 6A 62
Exmoor Rd. IP11: Fel 5A 62
EYKE 1H 25
Eyke Rd. IP12: Brom 4G 25

F

Factory La. CO11: Bran, Catt 6F 55
Fagbury Rd. IP11: Fel 1A 64
Fairbairn Av. IP5: Kes 2G 39
Fairfax Gdns. IP6: N Mar 4E 11
Fairfield Av. IP11: Fel 6B 62
Fairfield Hill IP14: S'ket 5D 6
Fairfield Rd. IP3: Ips 1F 45
Fairlight Cl. IP4: Ips 6F 29
Fairways, The IP4: Rus A 4B 38
Falcon Res. Trailer Pk.
    IP5: Mart H 1D 40
Falcon St. IP1: Ips 4B 36 (3D 4)
    IP11: Fel 5H 61
Falmouth Cl. IP5: Kes 3E 39
Faraday Rd. IP4: Ips 4E 37
Farina Cl. IP1: Ips 2G 35
Farlingayes IP12: Wood 4G 23
Farriers Cl. IP5: Mart H 1B 40
Farrier's Rd. IP14: S'ket 2C 8
Farriers Went IP11: T Mary 4G 61
Farthing Rd. IP1: Ips 2D 34
Farthing Rd. Ind. Est. IP1: Ips 2D 34
Farthings Went IP9: Cap 2E 51
Faulkeners Way IP11: T Mary 3E 61
Fawley Cl. IP4: Ips 2H 37
Fayrefield Rd. IP12: Mel 4B 24
Featherbroom Gdns. IP13: W Mar 6F 13
Feathers Fld. IP11: Fel 6G 62
Felaw St. IP2: Ips 5C 36 (6E 5)
Felbridge Ct. IP12: Wood 6G 23
Felix Cl. IP5: Kes 2E 39
Felix Rd. IP3: Ips 2G 45
    IP11: Fel 1G 65
    IP14: S'and 3G 7
FELIXSTOWE 1F 65
Felixstowe Beach Holiday Pk.
    IP11: Fel 3D 64
FELIXSTOWE FERRY 1G 63
FELIXSTOWE GENERAL HOSPITAL 1G 65
Felixstowe Rd. IP3: Ips 5E 37
    IP10: Lev 2B 46
    IP12: Mart 1C 40
Felixstowe Station (Rail) 6B 62
Fellbrig Av. IP5: Rus A 3C 38
Felnor Wlk. IP11: Fel 1F 65
Felsham Ct. IP14: S'ket 2F 9
Fen Alder Carr Nature Reserve 1D 10
Fenbridge La. CO7: E Ber 5G 53
Fen Bright Circ. IP3: Ips 4H 45
Fen Mdw. IP11: T Mary 3F 61
Fen Mdw. Wlk. IP12: Wood 1G 33
Fenn Cl. IP14: S'ket 2D 8
Fenn La. IP12: New 6H 41
Fentons Way IP5: Kes 2F 39
Fen Vw. IP8: Wash 3A 42
Fen Wlk. IP12: Wood 1G 33
Ferguson Way IP5: Kes 2E 39

Ferndown Rd. IP11: Fel 5D 62
Fernhayes Cl. IP2: Ips 1H 43
Fernhill Cl. IP12: Wood 4H 23
Ferry La. IP11: Fel 2A 64
    (not continuous)
Ferry Rd. IP11: Fel 5D 62
    IP12: Baw 1H 63
Fiddlers La. CO7: E Ber 2H 53
Field Vw. IP10: Buc 6H 47
Fife Rd. IP4: Ips 6G 29
Finbars Wlk. IP4: Ips 4D 36 (3H 5)
Finborough Cl. IP4: Rus A 3C 38
Finborough Rd. IP14: One, S'ket 5A 6
Finch Cl. IP14: S'ket 6H 7
Finchley Rd. IP4: Ips 3D 36 (1G 5)
Findley Cl. IP9: Sutt 6B 56
Finney's Drift IP10: Nac 6F 47
Fir Cl. IP13: W Mar 4F 13
Fircroft Rd. IP1: Ips 5H 27
Firebronds Rd. IP9: Holb 3F 57
Firmin Cl. IP1: Ips 3H 35
Fir Tree Hill IP9: Holb 3G 57
Fir Tree Ri. IP2: Ips 1D 42
Fishbane Cl. IP3: Ips 3F 45
Fisher's La. CO7: E Ber 2F 55
Fishpond Rd. IP12: Wald 3H 41
Fishponds La. IP9: Holb 3G 57
Fishponds Way IP14: Hau 1A 6
Fisk's La. IP1: Ips 4E 27
Fitness First Health Club 4A 4
Fitzgerald Ct. IP4: Ips 4F 37
Fitzgerald Rd. IP8: Bram 6B 26
    IP12: Wood 5H 23
Fitzmaurice Rd. IP3: Ips 6G 37
Fitzroy St. IP1: Ips 3B 36 (1D 4)
Fitzwilliam Cl. IP2: Ips 1G 43
    IP12: Wood 1F 33
Five Acres IP9: Holb 3F 57
Fiveways IP13: L Hac 3H 13
Flatford Bridge Cottage 6A 54
Flatford Cl. IP14: S'ket 2E 9
Flatford La. CO7: E Ber 5A 54
Flatford Rd. CO7: E Ber 4G 53
Fleetwood Av. IP11: Fel 6C 62
Fleetwood Rd. IP11: Fel 6C 62
Fletcher Rd. IP3: Ips 3E 45
Fletchers Cl. IP6: Barh 4C 16
Fletchers La. IP5: Kes 1H 39
Flindell Dr. IP8: Bram 5B 26
Flint Cl. IP2: Ips 1A 44
Flordon Rd. IP6: C Mary 2E 11
Foden Av. IP1: Ips 5D 26
Fonnereau Rd. IP1: Ips 2B 36 (1C 4)
Ford Cl. IP14: S'ket 1E 9
Fordham Pl. IP4: Rus A 4C 38
Ford Vw. Rd. IP14: S'ket 1E 9
Fore Hamlet IP4: Ips 4D 36 (4G 5)
Forest Cl. IP4: Ips 2F 37
Forester Cl. IP8: Ips 3F 43
Foresters Wlk. IP6: Barh 4C 16
Forest La. IP5: Mart H 3B 40
Fore St. IP4: Ips 4C 36 (3E 5)
Fore Street Swimming Pool 4F 5
Forfar Cl. IP4: Ips 6G 29
Forge Cl. IP10: Buc 5H 47
Fornham Ho's. IP4: Ips 3G 37
Foundation St. IP4: Ips 4C 36 (4E 5)
Foundry La. IP3: Ips 4B 36 (4D 4)
Fountains Rd. IP2: Ips 2G 43
Foxburrow Farm 1A 24
Foxburrow Rd. IP3: Pur F 2C 46
Fox Ct. IP14: S'ket 5E 7
Foxglove Av. IP6: N Mar 5D 10
Foxglove Cres. IP3: Pur F 2B 46
Foxglove IP11: Fel 6D 62
Foxgrove Gdns. IP11: Fel 6D 62
Foxgrove La. IP11: Fel 6D 62
Foxhall Cl. CO7: E Ber 1H 53
Foxhall Flds. CO7: E Ber 2H 53
Foxhall Heath Stadium 4D 38
Foxhall Rd. IP3: Ips 4E 37
    IP4: Ips, Rus A 5A 38
    IP10: Brig, Fox 4F 39
Fox Lea IP5: Kes 1H 39
Foxtail Rd. IP3: Ips 3A 46
Fox Way IP3: Ips 4B 46

Foxwood Cres. IP4: Rus A 4C 38
Framlingham Ct. IP1: Ips 1H 35
Frampton Rd. IP3: Ips 3F 45
Franciscan Way IP1: Ips 4B 36 (3C 4)
Francis Cl. IP5: Kes 1H 39
Franklin Rd. IP3: Ips 1G 45
Fraser Rd. IP1: Ips 2G 35
  IP8: Bram 4B 26
Freehold Rd. IP4: Ips 3F 37
  IP6: N Mar 2C 10
Freeman Av. IP6: Hen 2A 18
Freeman Cl. IP7: Had 2E 49
Freston Hill IP9: Fres 6D 44
Freston Rd. IP3: Ips 4H 45
Friars Bri. Rd. IP1: Ips 4A 36 (3B 4)
Friars Cl. IP11: Fel 5E 63
Friars Ct. IP12: Mel 4B 24
Friars Courtyard IP1: Ips 3C 4
Friars Rd. IP7: Had 3D 48
Friars St. IP1: Ips 4B 36 (3C 4)
Friends Wlk. IP5: Kes 1G 39
Fritillary Cl. IP8: Ips 3F 43
Fritton Cl. IP2: Ips 2H 43
Frobisher Rd. IP3: Ips 2D 44
Frog Hall La. IP7: Had 3F 49
Frogs All. IP9: S'ly 1F 59
Front Rd. IP3: Ips 3A 46
Fuchsia Rd. IP4: Ips 4F 37
Fullers Cl. IP7: Had 3F 49
Fullers Fld. IP6: West 3D 28
Furness Cl. IP2: Ips 3G 43
Fynn La. IP6: Tudd 2H 29
Fynn Rd. IP12: Wood 2E 33

G

Gaell Cres. IP7: Had 4E 49
GAINSBOROUGH 3G 45
Gainsborough La. IP3: Ips 3E 45
Gainsborough Rd. IP4: Ips 1C 36
  IP11: Fel .1F 65
  IP14: S'ket 5B 6
Gainsborough Sports & Community Cen.
  . . . . .3G 45
Gala Bingo .4G 35
Gallows Hill IP7: Had 2D 48
Gallows Hill Rd. IP7: Had 2C 48
Galway Av. IP1: Ips 6F 27
Gandish Cl. CO7: E Ber 4A 54
Gandish Rd. CO7: E Ber 4A 54
Ganges Rd. IP9: S Gate 6G 59
Gannet Rd. IP2: Ips 6F 35
Garden Cl. IP9: S'ly 3E 59
Garden Fld. IP11: Fel 6H 61
Garfield Cl. IP11: Fel 2E 65
Garfield Dr. IP11: Fel 2E 65
Garfield Rd. IP11: Fel 2E 65
  (not continuous)
Garrick Way IP1: Ips 4H 27
Garrison La. IP11: Fel 2E 65
Garrod App. IP12: Mel 1B 24
Garrods IP9: Cap 2E 51
Garrods, The IP5: Kes 3E 39
Gascoigne Dr. IP6: Hen 2A 18
Gaston End CO7: E Ber 2H 53
Gatacre Rd. IP2: Ips 2H 35
Gate Farm Rd. IP9: S Gate 5H 59
Gatekeeper Cl. IP8: Ips 3F 43
Gaye St. IP1: Ips 3A 36 (1A 4)
Gayfer Av. IP5: Kes 1A 40
Gayford Ct. IP7: Had 4E 49
Gaymers La. IP11: T Mary 3E 61
Generals M. IP11: Fel 6G 61
Geneva Av. IP5: Mart H 1D 40
Geneva Rd. IP1: Ips 3A 36 (1B 4)
George Frost Cl. IP4: Ips 2C 36
George La. IP13: W Mar 5F 13
George St. IP7: Had 3E 49
Georgian Ct. IP11: Fel 5A 62
Geralds Av. IP4: Ips 4F 37
Gibbons St. IP1: Ips 3H 35
Gifford Cl. IP9: Holb 3C 57
Giffords Pl. IP4: Rus A 3C 38
Gilbert Cl. IP6: N Mar 3C 10
Giles Ct. IP6: Cla 5D 16

Giles Way IP6: Wit 4F 19
Gippeswyk Av. IP2: Ips 5H 35 (6A 4)
Gippeswyk Rd. IP2: Ips 5A 36 (6A 4)
Gipping Pl. IP14: S'ket 3D 6
Gipping Rd. IP6: Gt Bla 4B 16
  IP14: S'and 1H 7
Gippingstone Rd.
  IP8: Bram 6B 26
Gipping Way IP8: Bram 5C 26
  IP8: Spro .3C 34
  IP14: S'ket 5D 6
Gipsy La. IP6: N Mar 2C 10
  IP12: Wood 4H 23
Gipsy Row CO7: Gt Wen 1A 50
Girton Cl. IP12: Wood 1E 33
Girton Way IP2: Ips 2G 43
Gladstone Rd. IP3: Ips 4E 37 (4H 5)
  IP12: Wood 6H 23
Glamorgan Rd. IP2: Ips 2A 44
Glanville Pl. IP5: Kes 3E 39
Glanville Rd. IP7: Had 5F 49
Glastonbury Cl. IP2: Ips 2G 43
Glebe Cl. IP8: Spro 3C 34
Glebe End IP9: Cap 1E 51
Glebe Way IP6: Barh 3D 16
Glemham Dr. IP4: Rus A 5C 38
Glemsford Cl. IP11: Fel 2C 64
Glemsford Ct. IP11: Fel 2C 64
Glemsford Rd. IP14: S'ket 1E 9
Glenavon Rd. IP4: Ips 2A 38
Glencoe Rd. IP4: Ips 6H 29
Gleneagles Cl. IP11: Fel 5D 62
Gleneagles Dr. IP4: Ips 4A 38
Glenfield Av. IP11: Fel 5B 62
Glenhurst Av. IP4: Ips 1G 37
Gloster Rd. IP5: Mart H 2C 40
Gloucester Ho. IP11: Fel 6H 61
  (off Walk, The)
Gloucester Rd. IP3: Ips 1F 45
Gobbitts Yd. IP12: Wood 6H 23
  (off Thoroughfare)
Godbold Cl. IP5: Kes 2G 39
Goddard Rd. IP1: Ips 4D 26
Goddard Rd. E. IP1: Ips 4E 27
Godfrey's Wood IP12: Wood 5H 23
Goldcrest Ct. IP2: Ips 6E 35
Goldcrest Rd. IP2: Ips 6D 34
Goldsmith Rd. IP1: Ips 3F 27
Golf Rd. IP11: Fel 6E 63
Gonville Cl. IP12: Wood 1F 33
Goodall Ter. IP5: Kes 1H 39
Goodman Gro. IP5: Kes 2H 39
Goodwood Cl. IP1: Ips 3A 28
Gordon Rd. IP4: Ips 2F 37
Goring Rd. IP4: Ips 3G 37
Gorsehayes IP2: Ips 6A 36
Gorse Rd. IP3: Ips 1G 45
Gosford Way IP11: Fel 5D 62
Gostling Pl. IP5: Kes 1H 39
Gowers Cl. IP5: Kes 2H 39
Gower St. IP2: Ips 5B 36 (5D 4)
Gowle Rd. IP14: S'ket 3C 6
Goyfield Av. IP11: Fel 1E 65
Grafton Way IP1: Ips 4A 36 (4B 4)
Graham Av. IP1: Ips 1A 36
Graham Rd. IP1: Ips 2H 35
  IP11: Fel .6A 62
Granaries, The IP6: Tudd 1H 29
Granary, The IP7: Had 4F 49
  (off Station Rd.)
Granchester Pl. IP5: Kes 2D 38
Grange Cvn. Pk., The CO7: E Ber 2E 55
Grange Cl. IP5: Kes 1A 40
  IP11: Fel .6H 61
Grange Ct. IP12: Mel 5A 24
GRANGE FARM 2F 39
Grange Farm Av. IP11: Fel 1C 64
Grange La. IP5: Kes 1A 40
Grange Rd. IP4: Ips 3D 36 (3H 5)
  IP11: Fel .2C 64
Grantham Cres. IP2: Ips 5H 35 (6A 4)
Granville Rd. IP11: Fel 2E 65
Granville St. IP1: Ips 3A 36 (1A 4)
Grasmere Av. IP11: Fel 5E 63
Grasmere Cl. IP3: Ips 3G 45
Gravel Pit La. CO11: Bran 3G 55

Grayling Rd. IP8: Ips 3F 43
Grays Cl. IP7: Had 2G 49
GREAT BEALINGS 1H 31
GREAT BLAKENHAM 3A 16
Gt. Colman St. IP4: Ips 3C 36 (2E 5)
Gt. Eastern Sq. IP11: Fel 6B 62
Great Fld. IP11: T Mary 3F 61
Gt. Gipping St. IP1: Ips 4A 36 (3B 4)
Great Harlings
  IP9: S Gate 5G 59
Great Tufts IP9: Cap 2E 51
GREAT WENHAM 1A 50
Gt. Whip St. IP2: Ips 5C 36 (5D 4)
Grebe Cl. IP2: Ips 1F 43
  IP14: S'ket 5A 6
Green, The IP7: Had 3F 49
  IP13: Grun 3F 21
  IP14: S'and 2H 7
Green Cres. IP10: Buc 6H 47
Green Dr. IP10: Fox 3H 47
Greenfinch Av. IP2: Ips 6E 35
Green La. CO7: Stra M, High 2B 52
  IP6: Tudd .3H 29
  IP6: Wit 4C 18
  IP12: Mart 5C 32
  IP13: Pett, W Mar 1F 15
Grn. Man Way IP12: Mel 5A 24
Grn. Oak Glade IP8: Ips 3E 43
Greens, The IP4: Rus A 5C 38
Greenspire Gro. IP8: Ips 2C 42
Greenways Cl. IP1: Ips 1A 36
GREENWICH 1D 44
Greenwich Bus. Pk. IP3: Ips 1D 44
Greenwich Cl. IP3: Ips 1D 44
Greenwich Rd. IP3: Ips 1C 44
Gresham Ct. IP1: Ips 1A 36
Gresley Gdns. IP2: Ips 6B 36
Gresswell Ct. IP5: Mart H 3C 40
Gretna Gdns. IP4: Ips 6G 29
Greyfriars IP1: Ips 3C 4
  IP12: Wood 2E 33
Grey Friars Rd. IP1: Ips 4B 36 (4C 4)
Greyhound Cnr. IP6: Cla 5D 16
Griffin Cl. IP2: Ips 6E 5
Grimston La. IP11: T Mart 3B 60
  (not continuous)
Grimwade St. IP4: Ips 4C 36 (4F 5)
Grindle, The IP8: Bram 2A 34
Grinstead Gdns. IP6: N Mar 5E 11
GRINSTEAD HILL 5E 11
Grinstead Hill IP6: N Mar 5E 11
Grosvenor Cl. IP4: Ips 1D 36
Grosvenor Ct. IP3: Ips 2G 45
Grove, The IP5: Mart H 1B 40
  IP12: Wood 6A 24
  IP14: S'ket 6E 7
Grove Cotts. IP1: Ips 5B 28
Grove Gdns. IP12: Wood 5F 23
Grove Hill IP8: Bel, Ips 5D 42
Grove Ho. IP8: Ips 2E 43
Grove La. IP4: Ips 4D 36 (3H 5)
  IP9: Chel .5B 58
Grove M. IP11: Fel 6A 62
Grove Rd. CO11: Bran 5G 55
  IP9: B'ley .5H 51
  IP11: Fel .5B 62
  IP12: Wood 5F 23
  IP13: Pett .6C 12
Grove Wlk. IP8: Ips 3E 43
GRUNDISBURGH 3F 21
Grundisburgh Rd. IP6: Tudd 1H 29
  IP12: Wood 6F 23
  IP13: Burg 1F 21
  IP13: Gt Bea 1F 31
  IP13: Has .4A 22
Guildhall 4D 48
Gull Cnr. IP13: Grun 2D 20
Gull La. IP13: Grun 2D 20
Gulpher Bus. Pk. IP11: Fel 3A 62
Gulpher Rd. IP11: Fel 5H 61
Gun Hill CO7: Ded, L'ham 6A 52
Gun La. IP11: T Mart 3D 60
Gurdon Rd. IP13: Grun 2G 21
Guthrum Rd. IP7: Had 3E 49
Gwendoline Cl. IP4: Rus A 5B 38
Gwendoline Rd. IP4: Rus A 5B 38

Gymnasium St. IP1: Ips 2A **36** (1A **4**)
Gymnastics Cen. 3G **45**

H

Hackney Rd. IP12: Mel 5A **24**
Hackney's Cnr. IP6: Gt Bla 3A **16**
Hackney Ter. IP12: Mel 5A **24**
HADLEIGH 3E **49**
Hadleigh Bus. Pk. IP7: Had 5H **49**
Hadleigh Hall IP7: Had 3D **48**
Hadleigh High Leisure Cen. 4G **49**
Hadleigh Ind. Est. IP2: Ips 3G **35**
Hadleigh Railway Wlk. IP7: Had 5G **49**
Hadleigh Rd. CO7: E Ber 2G **53**
   CO7: High 1A **52**
   IP2: Ips 4E **35**
   IP8: Spro, Ips 5B **34**
(not continuous)
Hadleigh Swimming Pool & Health Suite
   . . . . .3E **49**
Hale Cl. IP2: Ips 1E **43**
Halesowen Cl. IP2: Ips 3G **43**
Half Moon La. IP13: Grun 3G **21**
Halford Ct. IP8: Ips 1D **42**
Halifax Rd. IP2: Ips 1A **44**
Hall Farm Cl. IP12: Mel 3A **24**
Hall Farm Rd. IP12: Mel 3A **24**
   IP13: Gt Bea 1G **31**
Hall Fld. IP11: Fel 6G **61**
Halliwell Rd. IP4: Ips 3G **37**
Hall La. CO7: L Wen 1B **50**
   IP6: Cla 5F **17**
   IP6: Wit 4F **19**
   IP9: Cap .1B **50**
Hall Pond Way IP11: Fel 6G **61**
Hall Rd. IP14: S'ket 3B **6**
Halls Drift IP5: Kes 3E **39**
Hall Wlk. IP8: Bram 5A **26**
Halton Cres. IP3: Ips 2H **45**
Hamblin Rd. IP12: Wood 6A **24**
Hamblin Wlk. IP12: Wood 6A **24**
Hamilton Gdns. IP11: Fel 2F **65**
Hamilton Ho. IP4: Ips 2F **37**
Hamilton Rd. IP3: Ips 6G **37**
   IP11: Fel .1F **65**
Hamilton St. IP11: Fel 6H **61**
Hamilton Way IP14: S'ket 4D **6**
Hampton Rd. IP1: Ips 2G **35**
Handford Cut IP1: Ips 3H **35**
Handford Rd. IP1: Ips 3H **35** (2A **4**)
Hanover Ct. IP4: Ips 3D **36** (1H **5**)
Ha'penny Fld. IP9: Holb 3F **57**
Ha'penny Gdns. IP9: Holb 3F **57**
Harbour Vs. IP11: Fel 2G **63**
Hardwick Cl. IP4: Rus A 4B **38**
Hardy Cl. CO11: Bran 6F **55**
Hardy Cres. IP1: Ips 3G **27**
Harebell Rd. IP2: Ips 5G **35**
Hargrave Av. IP6: N Mar 5D **10**
Harkstead La. IP9: Wol 1H **57**
Harkstead Rd. IP9: Holb 4H **57**
Harrier Cl. IP3: Ips 2G **45**
Harrison Gro. IP5: Kes 1F **39**
Harrow Cl. IP4: Ips 4F **37**
Hartest Way IP14: S'ket 2F **9**
Hartley St. IP2: Ips 5B **36** (6D **4**)
Hartree Way IP5: Kes 2H **39**
Harvesters Way IP5: Mart H 3A **40**
Harvest Ho. IP11: Fel 1G **65**
Harvey's La. IP6: Barh 1F **17**
Hascot Hill IP6: Bark 6A **10**
HASKETON .3C **22**
Hasketon Rd. IP12: Wood 5F **23**
   IP13: Burg 2H **21**
Haskins Wlk. IP5: Kes 2H **39**
Haslemere Dr. IP4: Ips 3D **36** (1H **5**)
Hatfield Rd. IP3: Ips 5F **37**
Hatton Ct. IP1: Ips 2D **4**
Haughgate Cl. IP12: Wood 5G **23**
Haugh La. IP12: Wood 4G **23**
Haughley Dr. IP4: Rus A 3C **38**
Hauliers Rd. IP11: Fel 3C **64**
Haven Bus. Pk. IP11: Fel 3C **64**
Haven Cl. IP11: Fel 1C **64**

Havens, The IP3: Ips 4B **46**
Havergate Rd. IP3: Ips 3A **46**
Hawbridge IP9: Cap 1D **50**
Hawes St. IP2: Ips 6C **36** (6E **5**)
Hawker Dr. IP5: Mart H 1C **40**
Hawke Rd. IP3: Ips 2D **44**
Hawkes La. IP11: Fel 5G **61**
Hawks Mill St. IP6: N Mar 3D **10**
Hawthorn Cl. IP14: S'and 3G **7**
Hawthorn Dr. IP2: Ips 1D **42**
Hawthorn Pl. IP12: Wood 5F **23**
Hayhill Rd. IP4: Ips 2D **36** (1G **5**)
Hayman Rd. IP3: Ips 2E **45**
Haywards Flds. IP5: Kes 1G **39**
Hazelcroft Rd. IP1: Ips 5H **27**
Hazel Dr. IP3: Pur F 2B **46**
Hazelnut Cl. IP5: Rus A 6B **30**
Hazel Ri. IP6: Cla 5D **16**
Hazlitt Rd. IP1: Ips 4H **27**
Headingham Cl. IP2: Ips 1H **43**
Heath Cl. CO7: E Ber 2A **54**
Heath Ct. IP11: T Mart 1E **61**
Heather Av. IP3: Ips 6H **37**
Heather Cl. IP5: Mart H 3A **40**
Heathercroft Rd. IP1: Ips 4H **27**
Heatherhayes IP2: Ips 6H **35**
Heathfield IP5: Mart H 3A **40**
Heathfield M. IP5: Mart H 3A **40**
Heathfield Rd. IP9: Holb 3F **57**
Heathfields IP11: T Mart 1D **60**
Heathgate Piece IP11: T Mary 3F **61**
Heathland Retreat Cvn. Pk.
   IP4: Rus A 5B **38**
Heathlands Pk. IP4: Rus A 5B **38**
Heath La. IP4: Ips 4H **37**
Heath Rd. CO7: E Ber 2A **54**
   IP4: Ips 2H **37**
Heath Vw. IP5: Kes 3D **38**
Helena Rd. IP3: Ips 5D **36** (6G **5**)
Helston Cl. IP5: Kes 3E **39**
Henderson Cl. IP8: Bram 6B **26**
Hengrave Cl. IP2: Ips 1H **43**
Hening Av. IP3: Ips 3A **46**
HENLEY 2A **18**
Henley Av. IP1: Ips 4A **28**
Henley Ct. IP1: Ips 1B **36**
Henley Rd. IP1: Ips 3A **28**
(not continuous)
   IP6: Ake, Hen, Ips 2A **18**
Henniker Rd. IP1: Ips 1D **34**
Henry Rd. IP3: Ips 2G **45**
Henslow Rd. IP4: Ips 4G **37**
Henstead Gdns. IP3: Ips 1F **45**
Herbert Rd. IP5: Kes 1H **39**
Hereford Rd. IP6: Cla 4E **17**
Heron Cl. IP14: S'ket 5A **6**
Heron Rd. IP2: Ips 6F **35**
Hervey Cl. IP9: S Gate 5G **59**
Hervey St. IP4: Ips 2C **36** (1F **5**)
Hervey Ter. IP9: S Gate 5G **59**
Hessett Cl. IP14: S'ket 2F **9**
Hexham Cl. IP2: Ips 1H **43**
Heywood Cl. IP2: Ips 2F **43**
Hibbard Rd. IP8: Bram 5D **26**
Higgins Pl. IP5: Mart H 2B **40**
(off Drift, The)
HIGHAM 1A **52**
Higham Rd. CO7: High, Stra M 1A **52**
High Beach IP11: Fel 1H **65**
Highfield App. IP1: Ips 6G **27**
Highfield Dr. IP6: Cla 4E **17**
Highfield Rd. IP1: Ips 5F **27**
   IP11: Fel .1F **65**
   IP14: S'and 3G **7**
Highfields IP9: B'ley 5H **51**
High Hall Cl. IP11: T Mart 1D **60**
Highlands Cl. IP6: N Mar 3C **10**
Highlands La. IP12: Wood 5H **23**
Highlands Rd. IP7: Had 4E **49**
High Rd. IP11: T Mart, T Mary 1C **60**
High Rd. E. IP11: Fel 6C **62**
High Rd. W. IP11: Fel 6A **62**
High Row Fld. IP11: Fel 6D **62**
High St. CO7: Ded 6D **52**
   IP1: Ips 3B **36** (1C **4**)
   IP6: N Mar 3D **10**

High St. IP6: Tudd 2G **29**
   IP7: Had 3E **49**
   IP8: Spro .3B **34**
   IP11: Fel .4G **61**
   IP13: Uff 5D **14**
   IP13: W Mar 4F **13**
(Drift, The)
   IP13: W Mar 4F **13**
(Featherbroom Gdns.)
High St. M. IP7: Had 3E **49**
High Vw. Rd. IP1: Ips 6E **27**
Hildabrook Cl. IP2: Ips 2F **43**
Hilders Cl. IP9: S Gate 5G **59**
Hill, The IP6: Tudd 2H **29**
Hillary Cl. IP4: Ips 4F **37**
Hillcrest App. IP8: Bram 5C **26**
Hill Farm Bus. Pk. IP6: Wit 2F **19**
Hill Farm La. IP9: Chel 3C **58**
Hill Farm Rd. IP6: Play 3E **31**
   IP13: Grun 1E **21**
Hill Ho. La. IP6: N Mar 2C **10**
Hillhouse Rd. IP3: Ips 4D **36** (4H **5**)
Hill Ri. IP14: S'ket 2D **8**
Hill Rd. IP10: Fox 5H **39**
Hillside IP14: S'ket 2D **8**
Hillside Cres. IP3: Ips 6G **37**
Hill Vw. Bus. Pk. IP6: Cla 1E **27**
Hill Vw. Ter. IP12: Wood 6H **23**
Hilly Flds. IP12: Wood 1F **33**
Hilton Rd. IP3: Ips 2H **45**
   IP5: Mart H 1C **40**
Hines Rd. IP3: Ips 5F **37**
Hintlesham Cl. IP4: Rus A 4C **38**
   IP14: S'ket .2E **9**
Hintlesham Dr. IP11: Fel 6G **61**
Histon Cl. IP5: Kes 2C **38**
HMS Ganges Association Mus. 6H **59**
Hockney Gdns. IP3: Ips 3F **45**
Hodgkinson Rd. IP11: Fel 2B **64**
Hogarth Rd. IP3: Ips 2E **45**
Hogarth Sq. IP3: Ips 2E **45**
Hog's La. CO7: E Ber 5B **54**
Holbecks La. IP7: Had 4D **48**
HOLBROOK .3F **57**
Holbrook Cres. IP11: Fel 1C **64**
Holbrook Rd. IP3: Ips 2D **44**
   IP9: Sutt .6C **56**
Holcombe Cres. IP2: Ips 1E **43**
Holden Cl. IP2: Ips 6C **30**
(off Peppercorn Way)
Holfen Cl. IP12: Mart 5D **23**
Holkham Cl. IP4: Rus A 4C **38**
Holland Rd. IP4: Ips 3E **37**
   IP11: Fel .2E **65**
Hollingsworth Rd. IP14: S'ket 6E **7**
Hollow La. IP9: Chel 3C **58**
Holly Blue Cl. IP8: Ips 3F **43**
Hollybush Dr. IP11: Fel 4E **63**
Holly Cl. IP3: Pur F 2C **46**
   IP13: L Bea 2G **31**
Hollycroft Cl. IP1: Ips 4H **27**
Holly End IP5: Mart H 3A **40**
Holly La. IP5: Rus A 5B **30**
   IP8: Bel 4D **42**
   IP9: Sutt .5A **56**
   IP12: Mel .3H **23**
   IP13: L Bea 1F **31**
Holly Rd. IP1: Ips 2A **36**
   IP5: Kes .1C **38**
Holm Ct. IP5: Kes 1G **39**
Holm Oak IP9: Holb 2F **57**
Holst Mead IP14: S'ket 3C **6**
Holtonwood Rd. CO7: Stra M 1D **52**
Holt's La. IP6: C Mary 1G **11**
Holyoak La. IP14: Comb 4E **9**
Holyrood Cl. IP2: Ips 2G **43**
Holywells Cl. IP3: Ips 5D **36** (6H **5**)
Holywells Pl. IP3: Ips 2G **45**
Holywells Rd. IP3: Ips 5D **36** (6G **5**)
Homefield IP9: Cap 2E **51**
Homeorr Rd. IP11: Fel 1G **65**
Homer Cl. IP1: Ips 3G **27**
Honeysuckle Gdns. IP2: Ips 5F **35**
Hood Dr. IP6: Gt Bla 3A **16**
Hood Rd. IP3: Ips 2D **44**
Hook La. IP7: Had 5F **49**

Hope Cres. IP12: Mel 5H 23
Hop Mdw. CO7: E Ber 3G 53
Hornbeam Rd. IP14: S'and 3G 7
Horseman Ct. IP5: Mart H 2C 40
Horsham Av. IP3: Ips 6A 38
Hossack Rd. IP3: Ips 3F 45
Houghton Pl. IP4: Rus A 4C 38
House Martins, The *IP11: Fel* *5A 62*
(off Cage La.)
Howard Ho. IP2: Ips 6A 4
Howard St. IP4: Ips 2G 37
Howards Way IP5: Kes 1H 39
Howe Av. IP3: Ips 6H 37
Howlets Ter. IP9: Chel 3B 58
Howlett Cl. IP5: Kes 2H 39
Howlett Way IP11: T Mart 2E 61
Hoxne Cl. IP14: S'ket 2E 9
Hugh Ager Cl. IP14: S'ket 2D 8
Hughes Rd. CO7: E Ber 1F 53
Hulver Ct. IP3: Ips 1G 45
Humber Doucy La. IP4: Ips 4F 29
Hungarian Cl. IP13: Pett 3B 14
Hunt Cl. IP14: S'ket 2D 8
Hunter Rd. IP3: Ips 3H 45
Hunters End IP11: T Mary 4F 61
Hunters Ride IP5: Mart H 2C 40
Hurricane Pl. IP3: Ips 2G 45
Hurstlea Ct. IP6: N Mar 3D 10
Hurstlea Rd. IP6: N Mar 3C 10
Hutland Rd. IP4: Ips 2E 37
Hyams La. IP9: Holb 3E 57
IP9: Sutt 6B 56
Hyde Pk. Cnr. IP1: Ips 1B 4
Hyem's La. IP11: Fel 4C 62
Hyntle Cl. IP2: Ips 4F 35

I

Ickworth Ct. IP11: Fel 2B 64
Ickworth Cres. IP4: Rus A 4C 38
Iliffe Way IP14: S'ket 5D 6
Indoor Bowls 2G 37
Indoor Cricket Stadium 2A 28
Inkerman Cl. IP7: Had 3E 49
Inkerman Ter. IP7: Had 3E 49
Innes End IP8: Ips 1D 42
Inverness Rd. IP4: Ips 5F 29
IP Central IP4: Ips 3F 5
IPSWICH 3D 4
Ipswich Air Raid Shelter Mus., The 4E 37
IPSWICH CHILDREN'S HOSPICE 4H 37
Ipswich Crematorium IP4: Ips 1E 37
Ipswich Eastern By-Pass
IP5: Brig, Fox, Mart H 6B 32
IP10: Fox . . . . .3H **47**, 5G **47** & 6A **40**
Ipswich Golf Course 1C 46
Ipswich Hockey Club 5E 29
IPSWICH HOSPITAL 3H 37
Ipswich Mus. & Art Gallery 1C 4
IPSWICH NUFFIELD HOSPITAL, THE . . .5E 39
Ipswich Rd. CO7: Ded, L'ham 6A 52
(Gun Hill)
CO7: Ded, Stra M 6B 52
(Blackbrook Hill)
CO11: Bran 4G 55
CO11: Law 6F 55
IP6: Cla 5D 16
IP6: N Mar 4E 11
IP6: Wit 5F 19
IP7: Had 1G 49
IP9: Holb 1F 57
IP10: Nac 5C 46
IP12: New 6E 41
IP12: Wald 3G 41
IP12: Wood 3E 33
IP13: Grun 4F 21
IP14: S'ket 1E 9
Ipswich Southern By-Pass IP3: Ips 4C 46
IP8: Ips 3C 42
IP10: Buc, Fox, Nac 4F 47
Ipswich Sports Club 6B 28
Ipswich Station (Rail) 5A 4
Ipswich St. IP14: S'ket 5D 6
Ipswich Town FC 3A 4
Ipswich Transport Mus. 1H 45

Ipswich Western By-Pass
IP8: Ips, Wash, Spro, Bram 6B 34
Ireland Rd. IP3: Ips 2E 45
Iris Cl. IP2: Ips 4G 35
Irlam Rd. IP2: Ips 1E 43
Ivry Lodge *IP1: Ips* *2A 36*
(off Ivry St.)
Ivry St. IP1: Ips 2A 36

J

Jack's Grn. Rd. IP6: C Mary 1D 10
Jack's La. IP14: Comb 3A 8
Jackson Cl. IP5: Kes 2A 40
Jackson Ct. IP5: Mart H 2B 40
Jackson Way IP6: N Mar 4D 10
Jacobs Way IP12: Wood 6H 23
Jacqueline Cl. IP13: Grun 3G 21
Jaguar Cl. IP1: Ips 6D 26
James Boden Cl. IP11: Fel 6H 61
James Hatfield Ho. IP2: Ips 6E 5
Janebrook Rd. IP2: Ips 1F 43
Jasmine Cl. IP2: Ips 6G 35
Java Lodge Rd. IP13: Pett 2E 15
Jeavons La. IP5: Kes 2H 39
Jefferies Rd. IP4: Ips 3D **36** (2G **5**)
Jenners Cl. IP12: Mel 5A 24
Jennings Drift IP5: Kes 2G 39
Jermyns Cl. IP9: Cap 1E 51
Jervis Cl. IP9: Holb 3F 57
Jetty La. IP12: Wood 2H 33
Jewell Vw. IP5: Kes 2G 39
Jew's La. IP12: Mel 2C 24
Jimmy's La. CO11: Bran 3H 55
Johnson Cl. IP2: Ips 6B 36
John St. IP3: Ips 5D **36** (6G **5**)
John Swain Cl. IP6: N Mar 3C 10
Jordan Cl. IP6: C Mary 1E 11
Jordayn Ri. IP7: Had 3F 49
Josselyns, The IP11: T Mary 3F 61
Jubilee Av. IP14: S'ket 2D 8
Jubilee Cl. IP6: Cla 4D 16
IP11: T Mart 1E 61
Jubilee Ct. IP14: S'and 2H 7
Jubilee Cres. IP14: S'and 2H 7
Jubys Hill IP6: Wit 2F 19
June Av. IP1: Ips 5A 28
Jupiter Rd. IP4: Ips 2G 37

K

Karen Cl. IP1: Ips 6A 28
Keats Cres. IP1: Ips 4G 27
Keeper's La. IP11: T Mary 4D 60
Keightley Way IP6: Tudd 2G 29
Kelly Rd. IP2: Ips 4F 35
Kelvedon Dr. IP4: Rus A 4C 38
Kelvin Rd. IP2: Ips 6G 27
Kemball St. IP4: Ips 4F 37
Kempsters, The IP11: T Mary 4G 61
Kempton Cl. IP1: Ips 4A 28
Kempton Rd. IP1: Ips 4H 27
Kemsley Rd. IP11: Fel 6A 62
Kendal Grn. IP11: Fel 4E 63
Kennedy Cl. IP4: Ips 3F 37
Kennels La. IP13: Has 2D 22
Kennels Rd. IP10: Fox 1H 47
(not continuous)
Kensington Ct. IP14: S'ket 6D 6
Kensington Rd. IP1: Ips 1H 35
IP14: S'ket 6D 6
Kent Ho. IP11: Fel 5H 61
Kent Rd. IP14: S'ket 4C 6
Kentwell Cl. IP4: Rus A 5C 38
Kenyon Cl. CO7: Stra M 4C 52
Kenyon St. IP2: Ips 5B **36** (6D **4**)
Kerry Av. IP1: Ips 5E 27
Kersey Cl. IP14: S'ket 2E 9
Kersey Rd. IP11: Fel 1C 64
KESGRAVE .3F 39
Kesgrave Hall La. IP5: Kes 5H 31
IP13: Kes, L Bea 5H 31

Kesteven Rd. IP2: Ips 5A **36** (6A **4**)
Kestrel Dr. IP14: S'ket 6G 7
Kestrel Rd. IP2: Ips 6E 35
Keswick Cl. IP11: Fel 5D 62
Kettlebaston Way IP4: Ips 6C 28
Kettle La. IP6: C Mary 4G 11
Key St. IP4: Ips 4C **36** (4E **5**)
Keytes Way IP6: Gt Bla 3A 16
Khartoum Rd. IP4: Ips 2E 37
Kildare Av. IP1: Ips 5E 27
Kiln Bottom IP7: Had 1F 49
Kiln Cotts. IP14: S'ket 6C 6
Kiln Fld. IP11: Fel 6G 61
Kiln La. IP13: Gt Bea 1H 31
King Edward VII Dr. IP9: S Gate 6H 59
King Edward Av. IP13: W Mar 4F 13
King Edward Rd. IP3: Ips 6G 37
Kingfisher Av. IP2: Ips 6E 35
Kingfisher Dr. IP6: Gt Bla 3A 16
Kingfisher Way IP14: S'ket 6H 7
King George V Memorial Homes
IP3: Ips 6E 37
Kingpin Bowling Cen. 2C 40
Kings Av. IP4: Ips 4D **36** (3G **5**)
Kingsbury Rd. IP11: T Mary 4F 61
Kings Cl. IP12: Wood 1F 33
Kingsfield Av. IP1: Ips 1B 36
Kings Fleet Rd. IP11: Fel 2D 64
Kingsgate Dr. IP4: Ips 1E 37
Kingsland IP9: S'ly 4E 59
Kingsley Cl. IP1: Ips 4H 27
Kingsmead Cl. IP14: S'ket 4C 6
Kingsmead Rd. IP14: S'ket 4C 6
KINGSTON 3G 33
Kingston Farm Rd. IP12: Wood 2G 33
Kingston Rd. IP1: Ips 1G 35
IP12: Wood 1H 33
King St. IP1: Ips 3B **36** (2C **4**)
IP11: Fel 6H 61
King's Way IP3: Ips 1G 45
Kingsway IP12: Wood 6A 24
King William St. IP6: N Mar 3D 10
Kinross Rd. IP4: Ips 6G 29
Kinsey Vw. IP5: Kes 3E 39
Kipling Rd. IP1: Ips 4G 27
Kipling Way IP14: S'ket 3B 6
Kirby Cl. IP4: Ips 2F 37
Kirby Ri. IP6: Barh 4D 16
Kirby St. IP4: Ips 2F 37
Kirkham Cl. IP2: Ips 1H 43
Kirkton Cl. IP9: S Gate 5G 59
Kirton Rd. IP11: T Mart 1E 61
Kitchener Cl. IP2: Ips 1G 35
Kitchener Way IP9: S Gate 6G 59
Kittiwake Cl. IP9: Kes 6F 35
Knapton Ct. IP4: Ips 3D 4
Knights Cl. IP11: Fel 5E 63
Knightsdale Rd. IP1: Ips 6H 27
Knights La. IP5: Kes 2G 39
Knutsford Cl. IP8: Ips 2D 42

L

Laburnum Cl. IP3: Pur F 1B 46
IP8: Ips .1D 42
Laburnum Gdns. IP5: Rus A 6B 30
Lacewing Cl. IP8: Ips 3F 43
Lacey St. IP4: Ips 3D **36** (2G **5**)
Lacon Rd. IP8: Bram 5B 26
Lady La. IP1: Ips 2B 4
IP7: Had 2F 49
Lady La. Ind. Est. IP7: Had 1F 49
Lady Margaret Gdns.
IP12: Wood 1E 33
Lady Row IP9: S'ly 3E 59
Ladywood Rd. IP4: Ips 2H 37
Lagonda Dr. IP1: Ips 6D 26
Lake Side IP14: S'ket 5C 6
Lakeside Cl. IP2: Ips 1F 43
Lakeside Rd. IP2: Ips 1F 43
Lamberts La. IP5: Rus A 5H 29
Lambeth Cl. IP1: Ips 1H 35
Lambourne Rd. IP1: Ips 3A 28
Lanark Rd. IP4: Ips 6G 29
Lancaster Dr. IP5: Mart H 3C 40

Lancaster Ho. *IP11: Fel* 6H **61**
    (off Walk, The)
Lancaster Rd. IP4: Ips 3D **36** (2G **5**)
Lancaster Way IP6: Cla 4D **16**
Lancers, The IP12: Wood 2E **33**
Lancing Av. IP4: Ips 1F **37**
LANDGUARD COMMON 5C **64**
Landguard Ct. IP11: Fel 4D **64**
Landguard Cvn Pk. IP11: Fel 5D **64**
Landguard Rd. IP11: Fel 5D **64**
Landseer Cl. IP3: Ips 2F **45**
Landseer Rd. IP3: Ips 6D **36**
Lanercost Way IP2: Ips 1H **43**
Langdale Cl. IP11: Fel 5E **63**
Langer Pk. Ind. Est. IP11: Fel 2D **64**
Langer Rd. IP11: Fel 4D **64**
Langford Cl. IP14: S'ket 3B **6**
Langley Av. IP11: Fel 6H **61**
Langley Cl. IP11: Fel 6H **61**
Langstons IP11: T Mary 3G **61**
Lansdowne Rd. IP4: Ips 4F **37**
    IP11: Fel 5C **62**
Lapwing Rd. IP2: Ips 6E **35**
Larchcroft Cl. IP1: Ips 5A **28**
Larchcroft Rd. IP1: Ips 5H **27**
Larch Ho. IP11: Fel 1D **64**
Larchwood Cl. IP2: Ips 4D **34**
Largent Gro. IP5: Kes 1H **39**
Lark Cl. IP14: S'ket 6G **7**
Larkhill Ri. IP4: Rus A 4B **38**
Larkhill Way IP11: Fel 6G **61**
Lark Ri. IP5: Mart H 2B **40**
Larksfield Rd. IP9: Sutt 5C **56**
Larkspur Rd. IP2: Ips 6G **35**
Larksway IP11: Fel 2C **64**
La Salle Cl. IP2: Ips 6A **36**
Lattice Av. IP4: Ips 3H **37**
Laud M. IP3: Ips 1F **45**
Laud's Cl. IP11: T Mary 3E **61**
Laurel Av. IP5: Kes 2D **38**
Laurel Dr. IP6: Gt Bla 3B **16**
Laurelhayes IP2: Ips 6H **35**
Laurel Way IP6: Cla 5D **16**
Lavender Hill IP2: Ips 5G **35**
Lavenham Rd. IP2: Ips 4F **35**
Lavenham Way IP14: S'ket 1E **9**
Lawford Pl. *IP4: Rus A* 4C **38**
    (off Seckford Cl.)
Lawns, The IP4: Ips 1H **37**
Lawn Way IP11: Fel 6H **61**
Layham Gdns. IP14: S'ket 2F **9**
Layham Rd. IP7: Had 5E **49**
Leeks Cl. IP7: Had 2E **49**
Leeks Hill IP12: Mel 4A **24**
Lee Rd. IP3: Ips 6E **37**
Leeward Ct. IP11: Fel 6B **62**
Leggatt Dr. IP8: Bram 5B **26**
Leicester Cl. IP2: Ips 2G **43**
Leighton Rd. IP3: Ips 3F **45**
Leighton Sq. IP3: Ips 3F **45**
Lely Rd. IP3: Ips 3E **45**
Leopold Gdns. IP4: Ips 1G **37**
Leopold Rd. IP4: Ips 1F **37**
    IP11: Fel 1F **65**
Leslie Rd. IP3: Ips 2H **45**
LETHERINGHAM 1A **12**
Letton Cl. IP9: Cap 2D **50**
Levington La. IP10: Buc 6H **47**
Levington Rd. IP3: Ips 5F **37**
    IP11: Fel 4D **64**
Lewes Cl. IP3: Ips 6B **38**
Lewis La. IP9: Sutt 6A **56**
Lidgate Ct. IP11: Fel 1B **64**
Lilac Wlk. IP6: N Mar 5D **10**
Lime Cl. IP13: Uff 6D **14**
    IP13: W Mar 5F **13**
Limecroft Cl. IP1: Ips 4H **27**
Limekiln Cl. IP6: Cla 5D **16**
Lime Kiln Quay Rd. IP12: Wood 6A **24**
Limerick Cl. IP1: Ips 5F **27**
Limes, The IP5: Rus A 6A **30**
Limes Av. IP8: Bram 1H **25**
Limetree Cl. IP6: N Mar 4E **11**
Lime Tree Dr. IP3: Pur F 1A **46**
Lime Tree Pl. IP14: S'ket 6E **7**

Lincoln Cl. IP1: Ips 4A **28**
Lincoln Gdns. IP6: Cla 4D **16**
Lincoln Ter. IP11: Fel 2E **65**
Lindsey Rd. IP4: Ips 2H **37**
Lindbergh Rd. IP3: Ips 2H **45**
Lindisfarne Cl. IP2: Ips 2H **43**
Lindsey Way IP14: S'ket 2E **9**
Lingfield Rd. IP1: Ips 3A **28**
Lingside IP5: Mart H 3B **40**
Ling's La. IP9: Hark, Chel 6A **58**
Link, The IP9: B'ley 5G **51**
Link La. IP9: B'ley 5G **51**
Link Rd. IP9: Cap 2D **50**
    IP9: S Gate 5G **59**
Links Av. IP11: Fel 5B **62**
Linksfield IP5: Rus A 2B **38**
Linksfield Gdns. IP5: Rus A 2C **38**
Linnet Dr. IP14: S'ket 6G **7**
Linnet Rd. IP2: Ips 5E **35**
Lion Barn Ind. Est. IP6: N Mar 5E **11**
Lion La. IP6: N Mar 5E **11**
Lion St. IP1: Ips 3B **36** (2C **4**)
Lister Rd. IP1: Ips 6G **27**
    IP7: Had 4G **49**
LITTLE BEALINGS 3G **31**
Little Cft. St. IP2: Ips 6D **4**
Lit. Gipping St. IP1: Ips 3A **36** (2B **4**)
Little Gro. IP9: Cap 2D **50**
Little Gulls IP9: Cap 2C **50**
Little La. IP13: W Mar 4E **13**
LITTLE LONDON 5E **9**
Little Lumpkid IP7: Had 1F **49**
Little Orchard IP9: Holb 3F **57**
Lit. St John's St. IP12: Wood 6H **23**
Little's Cres. IP2: Ips 5B **36** (6D **4**)
Little Tufts IP9: Cap 2E **51**
LITTLE WENHAM 1A **50**
Lit. Whip St. IP2: Ips 6D **4**
Llewellyn Drift IP5: Kes 2F **39**
Lloyd Rd. IP9: S Gate 6G **59**
Lloyds, The IP5: Kes 2F **39**
Lloyds Av. IP1: Ips 3B **36** (2C **4**)
Locarno Rd. IP3: Ips 6G **37**
Lockington Cl. IP14: S'ket 6F **7**
Lockington Rd. IP14: S'ket 6D **6**
Lockington Wlk. IP14: S'ket 6D **6**
Lockwood Cl. IP12: Wood 6G **23**
Lodge Farm Dr. IP11: Fel 6D **62**
Lodge Farm La. IP12: Mel 2B **24**
Lodge La. IP6: Gt Bla 5B **16**
Lodge Rd. IP13: Gt Bea, L Bea 2H **31**
    IP13: Uff 5D **14**
Lombard Ct. IP4: Ips 2E **37**
London Rd. IP1: Ips 3H **35** (1A **4**)
    IP2: Ips 5F **35**
    IP8: Cop 3A **42**
    IP9: Cap 3E **51**
    (not continuous)
Lone Barn Ct. IP1: Ips 1E **35**
Long Bessels IP7: Had 3E **49**
Longcroft IP11: Fel 5H **61**
Long Fld. IP11: Fel 5G **61**
Longfield Rd. IP9: Cap 1D **50**
Long Perry IP9: Cap 2E **51**
Long St. IP4: Ips 4D **36** (4G **5**)
Lonsdale Cl. IP4: Ips 2E **37**
Looe Rd. IP11: Fel 6D **62**
Loraine Way IP8: Bram, Spro 2A **26**
Lotus Cl. IP1: Ips 6D **26**
Loudham Hall Rd. IP13: C Ash, Pett 1F **15**
Loudham La. IP13: Uff 6E **15**
Love La. IP7: Lay 4B **48**
    IP12: Mel 5A **24**
Lovers La. IP9: Hark 6A **58**
Lovetofts Dr. IP1: Ips 6E **27**
    (not continuous)
Lwr. Brook M. IP4: Ips 3D **4**
Lwr. Brook St. IP4: Ips 4B **36** (3D **4**)
Lower Cres. IP6: Barh 2B **16**
Lwr. Dales Vw. Rd. IP1: Ips 1H **35**
LOWER HACHESTON 3H **13**
Lower Harlings IP9: S Gate 6G **59**
LOWER HOLBROOK 6H **57**
Lower Ho. La. IP12: New 6F **41**
Lwr. Orwell St.
    IP4: Ips 4C **36** (4E **5**)

Lower Rd. IP6: Ake, West 2B **28**
    IP13: Grun .4G **21**
    IP13: Uff 1E **25**
LOWER STREET
    Colchester .1A **52**
    Ipswich 6C **56**
Lower St. CO7: Ded, Stra M 6B **52**
    IP8: Spro 2B **34**
    IP9: Sutt 6C **56**
    IP13: Gt Bea 2H **31**
Lwr. Ufford Rd. IP13: Pett, Uff 4F **15**
Low Rd. IP12: Eyk 6H **15**
    IP13: Has 3C **22**
Lowry Gdns. IP3: Ips 3F **45**
Lowry Way IP14: S'ket 4B **6**
Lucena Ct. IP14: S'ket 5C **6**
Ludbrook Cl. IP6: N Mar 3C **10**
Ludlow Cl. IP1: Ips 3A **28**
Luff Mdw. IP6: N Mar 3D **10**
Lugano Av. IP5: Mart H 1D **40**
Lulworth Av. IP3: Ips 6A **38**
Lumms Va. IP5: Kes 2F **39**
Lupin Rd. IP2: Ips 5F **35**
Lupin Way IP6: N Mar 5D **10**
Luther Rd. IP2: Ips 5B **36** (6C **4**)
Lydgate Rd. IP14: S'ket 4C **6**
Lyle Cl. IP5: Kes 2H **39**
Lyndhurst Av. IP4: Ips 4H **37**
Lynwood Av. IP11: Fel 6C **62**
Lyon Cl. *IP5: Kes* 1H **39**
    (off Howards Way)
Lysander Dr. IP3: Ips 3H **45**

M

Macaulay Rd. IP1: Ips 3G **27**
Mackenzie Dr. IP5: Kes 1E **39**
Magdalen Dr. IP12: Wood 2E **33**
Magdalene Cl. IP2: Ips 1G **43**
Magdalen Rd. IP7: Had 3E **49**
Maginley Cres. IP5: Rus A 3C **38**
Magpie Cl. IP8: Ips 1D **42**
MAIDENHALL .1H **43**
Maidenhall App. IP2: Ips 1A **44**
Maidenhall Grn. IP2: Ips 1A **44**
Maidenhall Sports Cen. 1B **44**
MAIDENSGRAVE 2F **33**
Maiden Way IP7: Had 3E **49**
Maidstone Rd. IP11: Fel 6H **61**
Main Rd. IP5: Kes, Mart, Mart H 1D **38**
    IP6: Hen 1A **18**
    IP6: Tudd 4F **29**
    IP6: West 4D **28**
    IP9: Chel 2A **58**
    (not continuous)
    IP10: Buc 5H **47**
    IP13: Hach, L Hac 3G **13**
    IP13: Pett 2E **15**
Mais Ct. IP2: Ips 1G **43**
Maitland Rd. IP6: N Mar 5D **10**
Major's Cnr. IP4: Ips 3C **36** (2E **5**)
Mallard Ct. IP2: Ips 6G **35**
Mallard Ho. Bus. Cen. IP13: L Bea 4G **31**
Mallard Way IP2: Ips 1F **43**
    IP14: S'ket 5A **6**
Mallowhayes Cl. IP2: Ips 6A **36**
Malmesbury Cl. IP2: Ips 2H **43**
Malting La. IP13: Grun 3F **21**
Maltings M. IP7: Had 4E **49**
Malting Ter. IP2: Ips 5C **36** (6E **5**)
Maltsters Wlk. IP14: S'ket 2C **8**
Malvern Cl. IP3: Ips 6G **37**
    IP5: Rus A .2C **38**
Malyon Rd IP7: Had 1F **49**
Manchester Rd. IP2: Ips 1E **43**
Mandy Cl. IP4: Ips 3F **37**
Mannall Wlk. IP5: Kes 1H **39**
Manning Rd. IP11: Fel 3E **65**
Mannings Family Fun Cen. 4E **65**
Mannington Cl. IP4: Rus A 4C **38**
Manningtree Rd. CO7: Ded 5F **53**
    CO7: E Ber .4B **54**
    IP9: Sutt 6A **56**
Manor La. IP9: Sutt 6A **56**

Manor Rd. IP4: Ips	1C 36
IP5: Mart H	1B 40
IP11: Fel	5D 64
IP11: T Mary	4E 61
IP13: Has	5D 22
Manor Ter. IP11: Fel	5D 64
Mansbrook Blvd. IP3: Ips	3H 45
Mansfield Av. IP1: Ips	5G 27
Manthorp Cl. IP12: Mel	3A 24
Manwick Rd. IP11: Fel	3E 65
Maple Cl. IP2: Ips	6H 35
Maple Gro. IP6: Barh	2C 16
Maple Ho. IP11: Fel	1D 64
Maple Rd. IP14: S'and	3G 7
Maples, The IP4: Rus A	1B 38
Marbled White Dr. IP8: Ips	3F 43
Marcus Rd. IP11: Fel	6E 63
Margaret Rd. IP14: S'ket	3C 6
Margaret St. IP11: Fel	6H 61
Margate Rd. IP3: Ips	6G 37
Margery Girling Ho. IP11: Fel	5D 62
Marigold Av. IP2: Ips	6F 35
Marina Gdns. IP11: Fel	3D 64
Maritime Ct. IP4: Ips	4C 36 (4E 5)
Market Hill IP12: Wood	6H 23
Market Pl. IP7: Had	4E 49
IP14: S'ket	5D 6
Marlborough Rd. IP4: Ips	4E 37
Marlow Rd. IP1: Ips	6E 27
Marriott's Wlk. IP14: S'ket	6D 6
Marshall Cl. IP5: Kes	1F 39
Marshalls Mdw. IP14: S'and	3G 7
Marsh La. IP9: S Gate	5H 59
IP11: Fel	3A 62
	(Gulpher Rd.)
IP11: Fel	2E 63
	(Rue's La.)
Martello La. IP11: Fel	6E 63
Martello Pl. IP11: Fel	6E 63
Martello Tower	
King Edward VII Dr.	6H 59
Marsh La.	5H 59
Martinet Grn. IP3: Ips	2H 45
Martin Rd. IP2: Ips	5B 36 (6C 4)
Martinsyde IP5: Mart H	1C 40
MARTLESHAM	6B 32
Martlesham By-Pass	
IP12: L Bea, Mart	3C 32
Martlesham Creek Ind. Est.	
IP12: Mart	4D 32
MARTLESHAM HEATH	2B 40
Martlesham Heath Aviation	
Control Tower Mus.	1A 40
Martlesham Rd. IP13: L Bea	4H 31
Marvens, The IP8: Wash	2B 42
Maryon Rd. IP3: Ips	3G 45
Masefield Rd. IP14: S'ket	3B 6
Mason Ct. IP6: Barh	4C 16
Masons Cl. IP4: Ips	3E 37
Masterson Gro. IP5: Kes	3F 39
Mather Way IP2: Ips	5C 36 (6E 5)
Matlock Cl. IP2: Ips	1D 42
Matson Rd. IP1: Ips	1G 35
Matthews Cl. CO7: Stra M	4B 52
Maude St. IP3: Ips	6G 5
Maudslay Rd. IP1: Ips	5D 26
Maybury Rd. IP3: Ips	2G 45
Maybush Cl. IP11: Fel	6D 62
Maycroft Cl. IP1: Ips	3H 27
Mayfield La. IP5: Mart H	3B 40
Mayfield Rd. IP4: Ips	2H 37
Mayfields IP5: Mart H	3B 40
Mayfly Cl. IP8: Ips	3F 43
Mayo Ct. IP1: Ips	5F 27
Mayors Av. IP1: Ips	1B 36
Mayors Wlk., The IP1: Ips	2B 36 (1D 4)
May Rd. IP3: Ips	1H 45
Mays Ct. IP11: Fel	2E 65
Meadow Cl. IP9: Chel	3C 58
IP11: T Mart	1E 61
Meadow Cres. IP3: Pur F	2C 46
Meadow Cft. IP11: Fel	2C 64
Meadow Shop. Cen., The IP14: S'ket	4H 7
Meadowside IP13: W Mar	4F 13
Meadowside Gdns. IP4: Rus A	1B 38
Meadows Way IP7: Had	3E 49

Meadowvale Cl. IP4: Ips	2E 37
Meadow Vw. IP6: N Mar	3C 10
IP10: Buc	5H 47
Medite Ho. IP3: Ips	4B 46
Medway Rd. IP3: Ips	1E 45
Meeting La. IP13: Grun	3F 21
Melbourne Rd. IP4: Ips	2A 38
Melford Cl. IP4: Rus A	4C 38
Melford Ct. IP3: Ips	4B 46
Melford Rd. IP14: S'ket	1E 9
Melford Way IP11: Fel	2B 64
Mellis Ct. IP11: Fel	6G 61
Melplash Cl. IP3: Ips	5B 38
Melplash Rd. IP3: Ips	5B 38
Melrose Gdns. IP4: Ips	1G 37
MELTON	4B 24
Melton Grange Rd. IP12: Mel	5H 23
Melton Hill IP12: Wood	6A 24
Melton Mdw. Rd. IP12: Mel	5A 24
MELTON PARK	1B 24
Melton Riverside Nature Reserve	4C 24
Melton Rd. IP12: Mel	5A 24
Melton Station (Rail)	4C 24
Melville Rd. IP4: Ips	4E 37
Menai Ct. IP1: Ips	2A 36
Mendip Dr. IP5: Rus A	3C 38
Meredith Rd. IP1: Ips	5F 27
Mere Gdns. IP4: Rus A	5C 38
Meriton Ri. IP7: Had	5G 49
Merlin Rd. IP2: Ips	6D 34
Merriam Cl. CO11: Bran	5G 55
Merrion Cl. IP2: Ips	1D 42
Mersey Rd. IP3: Ips	1E 45
Michael's Mt. IP13: L Bea	2G 31
Michigan Cl. IP5: Kes	2E 39
Mickfield M. IP11: Fel	6G 61
Micklegate Rd. IP11: Fel	3D 64
Middleton Cl. IP2: Ips	1E 43
Middleton Rd. IP6: Barh	4D 16
Mid Suffolk Leisure Cen.	4B 6
Milano Av. IP5: Mart H	1D 40
Milden Cl. IP14: S'ket	2E 9
Milden Rd. IP2: Ips	4F 35
Mildmay Rd. IP3: Ips	2F 45
Mill Cl. IP9: Cap	2B 50
IP11: Fel	2C 64
IP11: T Mart	1D 60
Millennium Way IP5: Kes	3H 39
Millers Cl. IP7: Had	3F 49
IP14: S'ket	2C 8
Millers Vw. IP1: Ips	2G 35
Mill Fld. IP8: Bram	5C 26
Millfield Av. IP14: S'ket	6C 6
Millfield Gdns. IP4: Ips	3F 37
Mill Hill IP9: Cap	1B 50
IP13: Burg	2G 21
MILL HILLS	6H 23
Mill La. CO7: Ded	6E 53
IP6: Barh, Hen	1G 17
IP6: C Pet	1H 9
IP6: Gt Bla	3A 16
IP6: N Mar	5E 11
IP6: Wit	4F 19
IP7: Ker	1A 48
IP8: Bram	5C 26
IP8: Wash	2A 42
	(not continuous)
IP11: Fel	1C 64
IP11: T Mart	1D 60
IP12: Mart	6C 32
IP12: Wood	6H 23
IP13: Has	3A 22
IP13: W Mar	5F 13
IP14: Comb	6A 8
IP14: S'and	3H 7
Mill Piece IP10: Nac	5E 47
Mill Pouch IP11: T Mary	3E 61
Mill Ri. IP9: Holb	3F 57
Mill Rd. IP12: New	6H 41
Mill Rd. Dr. IP3: Pur F	2C 46
Mills, The IP4: Rus A	1B 38
Mills Ct. IP6: Barh	4C 16
Mill St. IP14: S'and	4H 7
Mill Vw. Cl. IP12: Wood	6F 23
Milner St. IP4: Ips	4D 36 (3G 5)
Milnrow IP2: Ips	1D 42

Milton Rd. E. IP14: S'ket	5E 7
Milton Rd. Nth. IP14: S'ket	5E 7
Milton Rd. Sth. IP14: S'ket	6E 7
Milton St. IP4: Ips	2G 37
Minos Way IP1: Ips	1E 35
Minsmere Rd. IP3: Ips	3A 46
Misson Cl. CO7: E Ber	2E 55
Mistley Way IP12: Wood	5G 23
Mitford Cl. IP1: Ips	3H 27
Mitre Way IP3: Ips	5H 5
Moat Farm Cl. IP4: Ips	1E 37
MOATS TYE	6C 8
Moffat Av. IP4: Ips	6G 29
Monarch Way IP8: Ips	3E 43
Monastery Ct. IP7: Had	2F 49
Monks Cl. IP11: Fel	5E 63
Monks Ga. IP8: Spro	3B 34
Monmouth Cl. IP2: Ips	2A 44
Montague Rd. IP11: Fel	1G 65
Montana Rd. IP5: Kes	2D 38
Montgomery Rd. IP2: Ips	1A 44
Monton Ri. IP2: Ips	1E 43
Montrose Ct. IP3: Ips	5E 37
Monument Farm La. IP10: Fox	5E 39
Moore Rd. IP1: Ips	4G 27
Moorfield Cl. IP5: Kes	1F 39
Moorfield Rd. IP12: Wood	6F 23
Moor's Way IP12: Wood	6F 23
Morecambe Cl. IP4: Ips	2F 37
Morgan Ct. IP6: Cla	5D 16
Morgan Dr. IP1: Ips	6D 26
Morgan Mdw. IP14: Comb	3C 8
Morland Rd. IP3: Ips	3E 45
Morley Av. IP12: Wood	1G 33
Mornington Av. IP1: Ips	6G 27
Morris Way IP6: N Mar	4D 10
Mors End CO7: Stra M	3C 52
Moss La. IP6: West	3E 29
Mottram Cl. IP2: Ips	1D 42
Mountbatten Ct. IP1: Ips	2H 35
	(off Prospect Rd.)
Mount Dr. IP3: Pur F	2C 46
Mow Hill IP6: Wit	3F 19
Mowlands IP9: Cap	2E 51
Mulberry Gdns. IP6: Gt Bla	3B 16
Mumford Rd. IP1: Ips	1F 35
Munnings Ct. IP3: Ips	3G 45
Muriel Cl. IP7: Had	3F 49
Murray Rd. IP3: Ips	6F 37
Murrills Rd. IP3: Pur F	2B 46
Mus. of East Anglian Life	6D 6
Museum St. IP1: Ips	3B 36 (2C 4)
Mussiden Pl. IP12: Wood	6G 23
Myrtle Rd. IP3: Ips	5D 36 (6H 5)

N	
NACTON	6F 47
Nacton Cres. IP3: Ips	1G 45
Nacton Rd. IP3: Ips	5E 37
IP10: Buc	6G 47
IP11: Fel	4D 64
Nansen Rd. IP3: Ips	1G 45
Nash Gdns. IP3: Ips	3G 45
Naughton Gdns. IP14: S'ket	2E 9
Naunton Rd. IP12: Wood	6F 23
Navarre St. IP1: Ips	3B 36 (1D 4)
Naverne Mdws. IP12: Wood	6H 23
Nayland Rd. IP11: Fel	2B 64
Naylor Ct. IP14: S'ket	4B 6
Neale St. IP1: Ips	3B 36 (1D 4)
Neath Dr. IP2: Ips	2H 43
Needham Lake Nature Reserve	4E 11
NEEDHAM MARKET	3D 10
Needham Market Station (Rail)	4E 11
Needham Rd. IP6: Codd	4H 11
IP14: S'ket	1E 9
Needham Rd. E. Ind. Est. IP14: S'ket	2G 9
Nelson Rd. IP4: Ips	2F 37
Nelson Way IP12: Wood	4G 23
Nene Dr. IP3: Ips	4A 46
Neptune Marina IP3: Ips	5G 5
Neptune Sq. IP4: Ips	4F 5
Netherwood Ct. IP5: Mart H	3B 40
Netley Cl. IP2: Ips	3G 43

Newark Cl. IP2: Ips 2G **43**
NEWBOURNE 6H **41**
Newbourne Gdns. IP11: Fel 2C **64**
Newbourne Rd. IP10: Brig 5C **40**
 IP12: Mart, Wald 6E **33**
Newbourne Springs Nature Reserve . . .5H **41**
Newbourne Springs Nature Reserve Vis. Cen.
 . . . . .6H **41**
Newbury Ho. IP4: Ips 3G **37**
Newbury Rd. IP4: Ips 3G **37**
Newby Dr. IP4: Rus A 4C **38**
New Cardinal St. IP1: Ips 4A **36** (4B **4**)
New Cut IP7: Had 3F **49**
New Cut E. IP3: Ips 4B **36** (4D **4**)
Newell Ct. IP7: Had 4E **49**
Newell Rd. IP6: Cla 5D **16**
Newhaven Way IP7: Had 2F **49**
Newnham Av. IP12: Wood 1E **33**
Newnham Ct. IP2: Ips 2F **43**
Newquay Cl. IP5: Kes 3C **38**
New Quay Cl. IP12: Wood 6A **24**
New Quay La. IP12: Wood 5A **24**
New Rd. IP9: Holb 4H **57**
 IP11: T Mary 4F **61**
 IP12: Mel 2H **23**
Newry Av. IP11: Fel 1E **65**
Newson St. IP1: Ips 2A **36**
New St. IP4: Ips 4C **36** (4F **5**)
 IP12: Wood 6H **23**
Newton Rd. IP3: Ips 5F **37**
 IP14: S'ket, S'and 2D **6**
Newton St. IP4: Ips 3C **36** (2F **5**)
New Village CO11: Bran 6F **55**
Next Generation Club 4C **46**
Nicholas Rd. IP11: Fel 1B **64**
Nicholls Cl. IP13: Uff 6D **14**
Nightingale Cl. IP14: S'ket 6G **7**
Nightingale Rd. IP3: Ips 3F **45**
Nightingale Sq. IP3: Ips 3F **45**
Nine Acres IP2: Ips 3E **35**
Nock Gdns. IP5: Kes 3E **39**
Norbury Rd. IP4: Ips 1G **37**
Norfolk Rd. IP4: Ips 3C **36** (1F **5**)
Norman Cl. IP11: Fel 5E **63**
 IP12: Mel 5H **23**
Norman Cres. IP3: Ips 1F **45**
Normandy Cl. IP14: S'ket 2D **8**
Northcliffe Ct. IP11: Fel 6E **63**
 (off Maybush La.)
North Cl. IP4: Ips 1D **36**
Northgate Arts Cen. 6E **29**
Northgate Sports Cen. 6E **29**
Northgate St. IP1: Ips 3B **36** (1D **4**)
North Hill IP12: Wood 5G **23**
Nth. Hill Gdns. IP4: Ips 3D **36** (1H **5**)
Nth. Hill Rd. IP4: Ips 3D **36** (1H **5**)
North Lawn IP4: Ips 1G **37**
Norwich Ct. IP1: Ips 2H **35**
Norwich Rd. IP1: Ips 4F **27** (1A **4**)
 IP6: Barh, Cla 1B **16**
Notcutts CO7: E Ber 4B **54**
Nottidge Rd. IP4: Ips 3D **36** (2H **5**)
Nunn Cl. IP12: Mart 5C **32**
Nursery Wlk. IP11: Fel 6A **62**

O

Oak Cl. IP4: Rus A 2B **38**
 IP11: Fel 1D **64**
Oak Eggar Chase IP8: Ips 3E **43**
Oakfield Rd. IP8: Cop 5A **42**
Oak Gro. IP8: Spro 3B **34**
Oak Hill La. IP2: Ips 6A **36** (6B **4**)
Oak Ho. IP2: Ips 1E **43**
 IP6: Cla 5D **16**
 (off Alasdair Pl.)
Oak La. IP1: Ips 2D **4**
 IP10: Fox 3F **47**
 IP12: Wood 6H **23**
Oak La. Ct. IP12: Wood 6H **23**
Oaklee IP2: Ips 2H **43**
Oak Rd. IP14: S'and 3G **7**
Oaks, The IP5: Mart H 3A **40**
Oaksmere Gdns. IP2: Ips 1H **43**
Oakstead Cl. IP4: Ips 3F **37**

OAKS TYE 1A **48**
Oakwood Ho. IP5: Kes 2E **39**
Oban St. IP1: Ips 2A **36**
Observation Ct. IP1: Ips 4A **36** (3B **4**)
Odeon Cinema 2E **5**
O'Feld Ter. IP11: Fel 5D **62**
Offord Cl. IP5: Kes 3G **39**
Ogden Gro. IP5: Kes 3E **39**
Old Barrack Rd. IP12: Wood 2E **33**
Old Bredfield Rd. IP13: Uff 6C **14**
Old Cattle Mkt. IP4: Ips 3D **4**
Old Chu. Rd. IP12: Mel 2C **24**
 IP13: Mel 2C **24**
OLD FELIXSTOWE 5D **62**
Oldfield Rd. IP8: Ips 2C **42**
Old Foundry Rd. IP4: Ips 3C **36** (1E **5**)
Old Hall Cl. IP6: Hen 2A **18**
Old Hall La. IP9: B'ley 1H **51**
Oldhall Rd. IP9: S'ly 2F **59**
Old Kirton Rd. IP11: T Mart 1D **60**
Old London Rd. IP9: Cap 4C **50**
Old Maltings App.
 IP12: Wood 5A **24**
Old Maltings Cl. IP12: Wood 6A **24**
Old Norwich Rd. IP1: Ips 1E **27**
Old Paper Mill La. IP6: Cla 5D **16**
Old Rectory Cl. IP6: Barh 3D **16**
Old Rectory Wlk. IP9: Cap 2C **50**
Old School Ct. IP14: S'ket 5D **6**
Old School Ho. IP9: S Gate 6H **59**
Old School M. IP14: S'ket 5D **6**
Old St., The IP9: Cap 2E **51**
Olympus Cl. IP1: Ips 5D **26**
Onehouse La. IP1: Ips 6A **28**
Onehouse Rd. IP14: S'ket 5A **6**
Opal Av. IP1: Ips 6E **27**
Orchard Cl. IP12: Wood 4H **23**
Orchard End IP13: Grun 3G **21**
Orchard Ga. IP2: Ips 4D **34**
 IP6: N Mar 3D **10**
Orchard Gro. IP5: Kes 2D **38**
 IP6: Cla 6D **16**
Orchard Pl. IP13: W Mar 5E **13**
Orchard Rd. IP8: Bram 5B **26**
Orchard St. IP4: Ips 3C **36** (2F **5**)
Orchid Cl. IP2: Ips 5F **35**
Orchid Way IP6: N Mar 5D **10**
Oregon Rd. IP5: Kes 2D **38**
Orford Rd. IP11: Fel 4D **64**
 IP12: Brom 4D **24**
Orford St. IP1: Ips 2A **36** (1A **4**)
Orkney Rd. IP4: Ips 6F **29**
Orvis La. CO7: E Ber 4B **54**
Orwell Bus. Cen. IP3: Ips 1D **44**
Orwell Ct. IP12: Wood 2F **33**
Orwell Gdns. IP2: Ips 6H **35**
Orwell Hgts. IP2: Ips 1F **43**
Orwell Ho. IP11: Fel 1B **64**
Orwell Pl. IP4: Ips 4C **36** (3E **5**)
Orwell Retail Pk. IP2: Ips 4H **35**
Orwell Ri. IP9: Chel 2C **58**
Orwell Rd. IP3: Ips 5F **37**
 IP11: Fel 2E **65**
 IP14: S'ket 1D **8**
Orwell Vw. Rd. IP9: S'ly 3F **59**
Osborne Rd. IP3: Ips 5F **37**
Osier Cl. IP12: Mel 5A **24**
Otley Ct. IP11: Fel 6G **61**
Oulton Rd. IP3: Ips 6D **36**
Oxford Dr. IP7: Had 1E **49**
 IP12: Wood 2E **33**
Oxford Rd. IP4: Ips 4D **36** (3G **5**)
 IP5: Kes 2D **38**

P

Packard Av. IP3: Ips 1G **45**
Packard Pl. IP8: Bram 5C **26**
Padbrook Ct. IP9: Ips 4H **5**
Paddocks, The IP5: Mart H 1B **40**
 IP6: Tudd 2G **29**
Padstow Rd. IP5: Kes 3D **38**
Page Gdns. IP5: Kes 1H **39**
Page's Cl. IP14: S'ket 5C **6**
Paget Cl. IP6: N Mar 3C **10**

Paget Rd. IP1: Ips 2A **36**
Palfrey Hgts. CO11: Bran 5G **55**
Palmcroft Cl. IP1: Ips 4H **27**
Palmcroft Rd. IP1: Ips 4H **27**
Palmerston Rd. IP4: Ips 3D **36** (2G **5**)
Pannington Hall La. IP9: Wher 6G **43**
Paper Mill La. IP6: Cla 6C **16**
 IP8: Bram 2C **26**
Parade Rd. IP4: Ips 2E **37**
Pardoe Pl. IP4: Rus A 4B **38**
Park and Ride
 Bury Rd. 3E **27**
 London Rd. 1B **42**
 Martlesham 6A **32**
Park Av. IP11: Fel 6C **62**
Park Cl. IP5: Mart H 1B **40**
Park Ct. IP11: Fel 3D **64**
Parker Av. IP11: Fel 2A **64**
Parkers Pl. IP5: Mart H 1B **40**
Parkeston Rd. IP11: Fel 1C **64**
Parkins, The IP9: Cap 1E **51**
Parklands IP13: Uff 6D **14**
Park Nth. IP4: Ips 1C **36**
Park Rd. CO7: E Ber 2E **55**
 IP1: Ips 1B **36**
 IP6: N Mar 3D **10**
 IP13: Grun 4F **21**
 IP13: Leth 2A **12**
 IP14: Comb 4B **8**
Parkside Av. IP4: Ips 2C **36**
Parkside Offices IP3: Ips 5G **5**
Park Ter. IP12: Mel 1B **24**
Park Vw. IP11: T Mary 3E **61**
Park Vw. Rd. IP1: Ips 6H **27**
Parkway IP13: W Mar 4F **13**
Parkwood IP1: Ips 2B **36**
Parliament Rd. IP3: Ips 4G **37**
Parnell Cl. IP1: Ips 4G **27**
Parnell Rd. IP1: Ips 4G **27**
Parnham Pl. IP4: Rus A 4C **38**
Parsonage Cl. IP11: Fel 1C **64**
Parson's La. IP6: Bark 6B **10**
Partridge Ct. IP14: S'ket 5D **6**
 (off Violet Hill Rd.)
Partridge Rd. IP2: Ips 6E **35**
Pastures, The IP4: Rus A 4C **38**
Pattern Bush Cl. CO11: Bran 5G **55**
Patteson Rd. IP3: Ips 5D **36** (6G **5**)
Pauline St. IP1: Ips 5B **36** (6D **4**)
Paul's Rd. IP2: Ips 4G **35**
Peacock Cl. IP8: Ips 1D **42**
Peacock St. IP5: Kes 2H **39**
Pearce Rd. IP3: Ips 4F **37**
Pearcroft Rd. IP1: Ips 4A **28**
Pearl Rd. IP1: Ips 1E **35**
Pearse Way IP3: Pur F 2B **46**
Pearson Rd. IP3: Ips 6G **37**
Pearsons Pl. IP6: Hen 1B **18**
Pearsons Way IP8: Wash 2A **42**
Peart Gro. IP5: Kes 3G **39**
Peasey Gdns. IP5: Kes 3F **39**
Peel St. IP1: Ips 3B **36** (1C **4**)
Peel Yd. IP5: Mart H 1B **40**
Peewit Cvn. Pk. IP11: Fel 3D **64**
Peewit Rd. IP11: Fel 2C **64**
Peewit Hill IP11: Fel 2C **64**
Peewit Rd. IP2: Ips 6D **34**
Pelican Cl. IP2: Ips 6F **35**
Pembroke Av. IP12: Wood 1F **33**
Pembroke Cl. IP2: Ips 6A **36**
Pendleton Rd. IP2: Ips 2E **43**
Penfold Rd. IP11: Fel 1F **65**
Penn Cl. IP9: Cap 1E **51**
Penny La. IP3: Pur F 2C **46**
Penny Mdw. IP9: Cap 2D **50**
Pennypot CO7: Ded 6E **53**
Pennyroyal Gdns. IP2: Ips 5F **35**
Penryn Rd. IP5: Kes 3C **38**
Penshurst Rd. IP3: Ips 5A **38**
Penzance Rd. IP5: Kes 3C **38**
Peppercorn Way IP2: Ips 6B **36**
Pepper La. IP9: Wher 5A **44**
Pepper Pl. IP5: Kes 3G **39**
Perkins Way IP3: Ips 2E **45**
Pesthouse La. IP6: Barh 2B **16**
Peterhouse Cl. IP2: Ips 1G **43**

Peterhouse Cres. IP12: Wood 1E 33
Peter's Gro. IP9: Cap 1D 50
PETTISTREE 1E 15
Pheasant Ri. IP8: Wash 3A 42
Pheasant Rd. IP2: Ips 6F 35
Philip Av. IP11: Fel 2C 64
Philip Rd. IP2: Ips 5B 36 (6B 4)
Phillipps Rd. IP6: Barh 4D 16
Phillips Cres. IP6: N Mar 4E 11
Phipp Ct. IP1: Ips 3A 28
Phoenix Rd. IP4: Ips 2F 37
Picketts Rd. IP11: Fel 6D 62
Pickwick Rd. IP2: Ips 4F 35
Picton Av. IP1: Ips 6C 28
Pier Rd. IP11: Fel 5B 64
Pigeons La. IP8: Wash 1A 42
Pightle, The IP6: N Mar 3D 10
  IP9: Cap 1E 51
Pilbroughs Wlk. IP5: Kes 2G 39
  (Fairbairn Av.)
  IP5: Kes 2E 39
  (Twelve Acre App.)
Pilots Way IP12: Wood 1F 33
  (Portland Cres., not continuous)
  IP12: Wood 6G 23
  (Seckford Ter.)
Pimpernel Rd. IP2: Ips 6F 35
Pine Av. IP1: Ips 6A 28
Pine Bank IP5: Mart H 3A 40
Pine Cl. CO11: Bran 5G 55
Pinecroft Rd. IP1: Ips 5H 27
Pinecroft Way IP6: N Mar 4E 11
Pine Dr. IP3: Pur F 2C 46
  (not continuous)
Pine Gro. IP13: Grun 4G 21
Pine Ho. IP11: Fel 1D 64
Pines, The IP6: Cla 5D 16
  IP11: Fel 5F 63
Pine Tree Cl. IP5: Kes 2C 38
Pineview Cl. IP14: S'ket 6D 6
Pine Vw. Rd. IP1: Ips 6H 27
Pinewood IP12: Wood 2F 33
PINMILL 2C 58
Pinmill Cl. IP2: Ips 2D 42
Pin Mill Rd. IP9: Chel 3C 58
Pinners La. IP13: Has 5C 22
Pintail Cl. IP2: Ips 1F 43
Pipers Va. Cl. IP3: Ips 2D 44
Pipkin Hill IP7: Lay 6F 49
Pippins, The IP14: S'and 3H 7
Pipp's La. IP6: West 1D 28
Pitcairn Rd. IP1: Ips 1F 35
Pitts End CO7: E Ber 2A 54
Place Farm M. IP7: Had 2F 49
Platten Cl. IP6: N Mar 3C 10
Platters Cl. IP3: Ips 4G 45
Platters Rd. IP11: Fel 3D 64
Playfield Rd. IP9: Cap 2E 51
PLAYFORD 3E 31
Playford La. IP5: Rus A 6B 30
Playford Mt. IP13: Gt Bea 1E 31
Playford Rd. IP4: Ips 2A 38
  IP5: Rus A 5E 31
  IP13: L Bea 6E 31
Pleasant Row IP4: Ips 4C 36 (4E 5)
Plough Rd. IP9: Cap 2C 50
Plough St. IP3: Ips 5D 36 (5H 5)
Plover Rd. IP2: Ips 1F 43
Plummers Dell IP6: Gt Bla 3B 16
Plymouth Rd. IP11: Fel 5A 62
Pollard Ct. IP2: Ips 1E 43
Polstead Cl. IP14: S'ket 1F 9
Pond Cl. IP11: Fel 6G 61
Pond End IP6: Hen 1B 18
Pond Hall La. IP9: B'ley 2G 51
Pond Hall Rd. IP7: Had 4G 49
Poole Cl. IP3: Ips 6A 38
Poplar Cl. IP6: Cla 5D 16
Poplar Hill IP14: S'ket 3C 8
Poplar La. IP8: Wash 6C 34
Poplars, The CO11: Bran 3G 55
Poppy Cl. IP2: Ips 5G 35
Portal Av. IP5: Mart H 6B 32
Porter Rd. IP3: Pur F 2C 46
Portland Cres. IP12: Wood 1F 33
Portman Road 4A 36 (3A 4)

Portman Rd. IP1: Ips 3A 36 (2B 4)
Portman's Wlk. IP1: Ips 4H 35
Port of Felixstowe Rd. IP11: Fel 6F 61
PORT OF FLEXISTOWE, THE 2B 64
Post Mill Cl. IP4: Ips 3E 37 (1H 5)
  IP13: Grun 4F 21
Post Mill Cres. IP13: Grun 4F 21
Post Mill Gdns. IP13: Grun 4F 21
Post Mill Orchard IP13: Grun 4F 21
Post Office Cnr. IP9: Sutt 6C 56
Post Office La. IP12: Mart 4D 32
POTASH 3H 51
Potash La. IP9: B'ley 3H 51
Potters App. IP5: Kes 3E 39
Pound La. IP7: Had 3E 49
  IP8: Bram 3E 39
  (Loraine Way)
  IP8: Bram 5B 26
  (Street, The)
  IP8: Cop 4A 42
  IP9: Cap 2C 50
  IP14: S'ket 4D 6
Powling Rd. IP3: Ips 1F 45
Prentice Rd. IP14: S'ket 5E 7
Prentices La. IP12: Wood 5E 23
Presmere Rd. IP13: Pett 2D 14
Preston Dr. IP1: Ips 5G 27
Prestwick Av. IP11: Fel 5D 62
Pretyman Rd. IP3: Ips 6G 37
  IP11: Fel 4D 64
Priestly Cl. IP14: S'ket 3B 6
Priestly Rd. IP6: N Mar 4D 10
Primrose Hill IP2: Ips 5G 35
  IP9: Holb 4F 57
Primrose Way IP6: N Mar 5D 10
Princedale Cl. IP1: Ips 6H 27
Princel La. CO7: Ded 6E 53
Princel M. CO7: Ded 6E 53
Prince of Wales Dr. IP2: Ips 1H 43
Princes Gdns. IP11: Fel 1E 65
Princes Rd. IP11: Fel 2E 65
Princes St. IP1: Ips 2C 4
  IP1: Ips 5A 36 (5A 4)
Princethorpe Rd. IP3: Ips 5H 37
PRIORY HEATH 2H 45
Priory Rd. IP11: Fel 6D 62
Prittlewell Cl. IP2: Ips 2G 43
Private Rd. IP12: Mart 5C 32
Prospect Pl. IP7: Mel 5A 24
Prospect Rd. IP1: Ips 3H 35
Prospect St. IP1: Ips 2H 35
Providence La. IP1: Ips 6E 5
Providence St. IP1: Ips 3B 36 (2C 4)
Puffin Ct. IP14: S'ket 5G 7
Pump St. IP6: N Mar 4E 11
Punchard Way IP11: T Mary 3F 61
Purcell Rd. IP14: S'ket 3B 6
Purdis Av. IP3: Pur F 2C 46
PURDIS FARM 1C 46
Purdis Farm La. IP3: Fox, Pur F 1B 46
Purdis Rd. IP10: Fox 1F 47
Purplett Ho. IP2: Ips 6E 5
Purplett St. IP2: Ips 5C 36 (6E 5)
Put Hawks La. IP6: Bark 6C 10
Pykenham Way IP7: Had 3E 49
Pytches Cl. IP12: Mel 5H 23
Pytches Rd. IP12: Wood 5H 23

Q

QM Ind. Pk. IP3: Ips 2H 45
Q Tower 2E 65
  (off Garfield Cl.)
Quadling St. IP1: Ips 4B 36 (4C 4)
Quadrangle Cen., The IP3: Ips 1H 45
Quantock Cl. IP5: Rus A 2C 38
Quantril Ter. IP5: Kes 3G 39
Quay Side IP12: Wood 1H 33
Quay St. IP12: Wood 1H 33
Quebec Dr. IP5: Kes 1E 39
Queech, The IP9: Cap 1E 51
  (off Thorney Rd.)
Queens Av. IP12: Wood 1F 33
Queensberry Rd. IP3: Ips 2F 45
Queenscliffe Rd. IP2: Ips 6H 35 (6A 4)

Queen's Cl. IP14: Comb 5A 8
Queensdale Cl. IP1: Ips 6A 28
Queensgate Dr. IP4: Ips 1E 37
Queen's Head La. IP12: Wood 6G 23
Queensland IP9: S'ly 4E 59
Queens Rd. IP11: Fel 2F 65
Queens Row IP7: Had 4E 49
Queen's Sq. IP3: Ips 5G 45
Queen St. IP1: Ips 4B 36 (3C 4)
  IP7: Had 3E 49
  IP11: Fel 6H 61
Queen's Way IP3: Ips 1G 45
Queen Victoria Dr.
  IP9: S Gate 6G 59
Quentin Cl. IP1: Ips 1F 35
Quilter Dr. IP8: Ips 3D 42
Quilter Rd. IP11: Fel 1G 65
Quince Cl. CO11: Bran 4G 55
Quinton Rd. IP6: N Mar 4C 10
Quinton's La. IP1: Ips 5C 62
  (Links Av., not continuous)
  IP11: Fel 6D 62
  (Looe Rd.)
Quintons Rd. CO7: E Ber 2H 53
Quoits Fld. IP6: Cla 5D 16

R

RACECOURSE 6H 37
Rachel Ct. IP4: Ips 3D 36 (1F 5)
Radcliffe Dr. IP2: Ips 1D 42
Raeburn Rd. IP3: Ips 2E 45
Raeburn Rd. Sth. IP3: Ips 3D 44
Rampling Cl. IP7: Had 2E 49
Ramsey Cl. IP2: Ips 2H 43
Ramsey Rd. IP7: Had 2G 49
Ramsgate Dr. IP3: Ips 6G 37
Randall Cl. IP5: Kes 2H 39
Randolph Cl. IP4: Ips 4G 37
Rands Way IP3: Ips 4G 37
Randwell Cl. IP4: Ips 4G 37
Ranelagh Rd. IP2: Ips 4G 35 (5A 4)
  IP11: Fel 1F 65
Ransome Cl. IP8: Spro 3B 34
Ransome Cres. IP3: Ips 1G 45
Ransome Rd. IP3: Ips 1G 45
Ransomes Europark IP3: Ips 3B 46
Ransomes Ind. Pk. IP3: Ips 3B 46
Ransomes Way IP3: Ips 3A 46
Ransom Rd. IP12: Wood 5F 23
Ranson Rd. IP6: N Mar 4C 10
Rapier St. IP2: Ips 6C 36
Rattlesden Cl. IP14: S'ket 2D 8
Ravensfield Rd. IP1: Ips 6F 27
Ravens La. IP8: Bram 5B 26
Ravens Way IP12: Mart 5C 32
Ravenswood Way IP3: Ips 3G 45
Raven Way IP7: Had 5E 49
Raydon Cft. IP14: S'ket 2F 9
Rayleigh Rd. IP1: Ips 6F 27
Rayment Drift IP5: Kes 2F 39
Reade Rd. IP9: Holb 2F 57
Reading Rd. IP4: Ips 2G 37
Recreation Cl. IP11: Fel 5A 62
Recreation La. IP11: Fel 5A 62
Recreation Rd. IP14: S'ket 5C 6
Recreation Way IP3: Ips 1H 45
Rectory Fld. IP9: Chel 3B 58
Rectory Hill CO7: E Ber 4H 53
Rectory La. CO11: Bran 4H 55
Rectory Rd. IP2: Ips 6B 36 (6C 4)
Redan St. IP1: Ips 2A 36
Red Barn Piece IP13: Grun 4G 21
Rede La. IP6: Barh, Cla, Hen 4G 17
Redgate La. IP9: Wher 6B 44
Red Hall Ct. IP11: Fel 1H 65
Red Hill Rd. IP7: Aldh 1F 49
  (not continuous)
Red Ho. Cl. IP11: T Mart 1D 60
Red La. IP9: Cap 3D 50
Red Sleeve IP9: Cap 2C 50
Red Willows Trad. Est. IP14: One 5A 6
Redwing Cl. IP2: Ips 6E 35
Redwood Cl. IP12: Mart 4D 32
Reedland Way IP11: Fel 6G 61

Reeds Way IP14: S'and 2H 7
Reeve Gdns. IP5: Kes 1F 39
Reeve Lodge IP11: T Mart 2D 60
Regal Theatre .6E 7
Regent St. IP4: Ips 4D 36 (2G 5)
 IP14: S'ket 4D 6
Regent Theatre 2F 5
Regina Cl. IP4: Ips 4G 37
Reigate Cl. IP3: Ips 6G 37
Rembrow Rd. IP9: Cap 2C 50
Rendall La. IP14: S'and 1H 7
Rendlesham Ct. IP1: Ips 2H 35
 (off Beaufort St.)
Rendlesham Rd. IP1: Ips 2H 35
 IP11: Fel 6G 61
Renfrew Rd. IP4: Ips 1G 37
Reydon Ho. IP3: Ips 1F 45
Reynolds Av. IP3: Ips 3F 45
Reynolds Ct. IP11: Fel 6G 61
Reynolds Rd. IP3: Ips 2F 45
Riby Rd. IP11: Fel 2E 65
Richards Dr. IP13: L Bea 2G 31
Richardson Rd. CO7: E Ber 2A 54
Richardsons La. IP9: Chel 3A 58
Richmond Ho. IP4: Ips 3F 5
Richmond Rd. IP1: Ips 2G 35
Ridgeway IP14: S'ket 5B 6
Riley Cl. IP1: Ips 6D 26
Ringham Rd. IP4: Ips 3F 37
Risby Cl. IP4: Ips 3G 37
Ritabrook Rd. IP2: Ips 2F 43
River Gdns. IP14: S'ket 1E 9
River Hill IP8: Bram 1D 34
Riverside IP13: Has 4B 22
Riverside Ind. Est. IP13: W Mar 4F 13
Riverside Ind. Pk. IP2: Ips 6C 36
Riverside Rd. IP1: Ips 2F 35
Riverside Theatre 1H 33
Riverside Vw. IP13: W Mar 4F 13
Rivers St. IP4: Ips 2E 37
Riverview IP12: Mel 4B 24
River Wall IP12: Wood 1H 33
Rixon Cl. IP12: Mel 1B 24
Robeck Rd. IP3: Ips 2D 44
Robin Cl. IP14: S'ket 6G 7
Robin Dr. IP2: Ips 6E 35
Rodney Ct. IP12: Wood 4G 23
Rogers Cl. IP11: Fel 5A 62
Rogue's La. IP13: Pett 6E 13
Roma Av. IP5: Mart H 1D 40
Roman Way IP11: Fel 5E 63
Romney Rd. IP3: Ips 3F 45
Roper Ct. IP3: Ips 4H 37
Ropes Dr. IP5: Kes 1E 39
Rope Wlk. IP4: Ips 4C 36 (3F 5)
Rosebery Ct. IP11: Fel 3E 65
Rosebery Rd. IP4: Ips 4E 37 (3H 5)
 IP11: Fel .1G 65
Rose Ct. IP9: S'ly 3F 59
Rosecroft Rd. IP1: Ips 5H 27
Rose Farm Cvn. Site IP9: S Gate 5F 59
ROSE HILL 5F 37
Rose Hill IP6: Wit 6E 19
 IP13: Grun .2F 21
Rosehill Cres. IP3: Ips 5E 37 (5H 5)
Rosehill Rd. IP3: Ips 5E 37
Rose La. IP1: Ips 4B 36 (3D 4)
Rosemary Av. IP11: Fel 5C 62
Rosemary La. IP4: Ips 4B 36 (3D 4)
Rosery La. IP13: Gt Bea 1A 32
Rose Wlk. IP6: N Mar 5D 10
Ross Rd. IP4: Ips 6G 29
Roundridge Rd. IP9: Cap 1E 51
Roundwood Rd. IP4: Ips 2F 37
Rousies Cl. IP7: Had 3F 49
Routh Av. IP3: Pur F 2C 46
Row, The CO7: Stra M 3B 52
Rowan Cl. IP3: Pur F 1A 46
Rowanhayes Cl. IP2: Ips 6A 36
Rowarth Av. IP5: Kes 2F 39
Rowland Ho. IP11: Fel 6G 61
 (off Winston Cl.)
Rowley Cl. CO11: Bran 5G 55
Roxburgh Rd. IP4: Ips 6G 29
Royal Sq. CO7: Ded 6E 53
Roy Av. IP3: Ips 4G 37

Roy Cl. IP5: Kes 2E 39
Royston Dr. IP2: Ips 1E 43
Rubens Rd. IP3: Ips 2F 45
Rudlands IP8: Ips 2D 42
Rue's La. IP11: Fel 3D 62
Runnacles Way IP11: Fel 6G 61
Rushbury Cl. IP4: Ips 1G 37
Rush Cl. IP4: Rus A 5B 38
Rush Ct. IP5: Kes 1H 39
 (off Howards Way)
Rushmeadow Way IP11: Fel 4E 63
Rushmere Rd. IP4: Ips 2F 37
RUSHMERE ST ANDREW 2C 38
RUSHMERE STREET 6B 30
Rushmere St. IP5: Rus A 1A 38
Ruskin Cl. IP14: S'ket 3B 6
Ruskin Rd. IP4: Ips 4E 37
Russell Cl. IP12: Wood 5F 23
Russell Ct. IP11: Fel 4D 64
Russell Rd. IP1: Ips 4A 36 (4A 4)
Rydal Av. IP11: Fel 4E 63
Rydal Cl. IP14: S'ket 5B 6
Rydal Wlk. IP3: Ips 1H 45
Rye Cl. IP3: Ips 5A 38
Rylands IP9: Cap 1D 50

S

Saddlemakers La. IP12: Mel 2A 24
Saddlers Mdw. IP13: Grun 2G 21
Saddlers Pl. IP5: Mart H 2B 40
Sagehayes Cl. IP2: Ips 6A 36
St Agnes Way IP5: Kes 3C 38
St Andrew's Chu. Cl. IP5: Rus A 6A 30
St Andrew's Cl. IP4: Ips 4A 38
 IP12: Mel .3C 24
St Andrew's Dr. IP9: Chel 3B 58
St Andrew's Pl. IP12: Mel 3B 24
St Andrew's Rd. IP11: Fel 6B 62
St Annes Cl. IP12: Wood 2E 33
St Aubyns Rd. IP4: Ips 4F 37
St Audrys La. IP12: Mel 2B 24
St Audrys Pk. Rd. IP12: Mel 1B 24
St Audrys Rd. IP12: Mel 2B 24
St Augustine Rd. IP3: Ips 5A 38
St Augustine's Gdns. IP3: Ips 6H 37
St Austell Cl. IP5: Kes 3D 38
St Catherine's Ct. IP2: Ips 2F 43
St Clements Chu. La. IP4: Ips . . .4C 36 (4F 5)
ST CLEMENT'S HOSPITAL 5H 37
St David's Rd. IP3: Ips 6G 37
St Edmundsbury Ho. IP1: Ips 3E 37
St Edmunds Cl. IP12: Brom 3F 25
 IP12: Wood 1F 33
St Edmund's Pl. IP1: Ips 1B 36
St Edmunds Rd. IP1: Ips 1A 36
 IP11: Fel 3D 64
 IP14: S'ket 4C 6
ST ELIZABETH HOSPICE 4H 37
St Francis Ho. IP1: Ips 3C 4
St George's Ct. IP1: Ips 1C 4
St George's Rd. IP11: Fel 5D 62
St George's St. IP1: Ips 3B 36 (1C 4)
St Gotthards Av. IP5: Mart H 1D 40
St Helen's Chu. La. IP4: Ips 3D 36 (2G 5)
St Helen's St. IP4: Ips 3C 36 (2E 5)
St Isidores IP5: Kes 2H 39
St Ives Cl. IP5: Kes 3D 38
St John's Ct. IP4: Ips 3G 37
 IP11: Fel 1E 65
St John's Hill IP12: Wood 6H 23
St John's Rd. IP4: Ips 3E 37
St John's St. IP12: Wood 6H 23
St John's Ter. IP12: Wood 6H 23
St Lawrence Grn. IP5: Kes 1E 39
St Lawrence St. IP1: Ips 3B 36 (2D 4)
St Lawrence Way IP5: Kes 1E 39
St Margaret's Grn. IP4: Ips 3C 36 (1E 5)
St Margaret's Plain IP4: Ips 3C 36 (1E 5)
St Margaret's St. IP4: Ips 3C 36 (2E 5)
St Martins Ct. IP5: Kes 2H 39
St Martins Grn. IP11: T Mart 1E 61

St Mary Elms Chu. Path IP1: Ips 2C 4
St Mary's Cl. IP8: Bram 6C 26
 IP11: T Mary 4E 61
St Mary's Ct. IP1: Ips 2C 4
St Mary's Cres. IP11: Fel 5H 61
St Marys Dr. IP6: Play 3E 31
St Mary's Gdns. IP6: C Mary 2E 11
St Marys Pk. IP10: Buc 6H 47
St Marys Rd. IP4: Ips 2E 37
 IP6: C Mary 3D 10
 IP14: S'ket 4B 6
St Marys Way IP6: West 3E 29
St Matthew's Chu. La. IP1: Ips 1B 4
St Matthew's Ho. IP1: Ips 1B 4
St Matthew's St. IP1: Ips 3A 36 (1B 4)
St Michael's Cl. IP5: Kes 3D 38
St Nicholas Ct. IP1: Ips 3C 4
St Nicholas St. IP1: Ips 4B 36 (3C 4)
St Olaves Rd. IP5: Kes 1F 39
St Osyth Cl. IP2: Ips 3G 43
St Peter's Av. IP6: Cla 4C 16
St Peter's Cl. IP6: Cla 4C 16
 IP6: Hen 2A 18
 IP12: Wood 1E 33
 IP14: S'ket 5B 6
St Peter's Ct. IP6: Cla 4D 16
St Peter's Quay IP3: Ips 4E 5
St Peter's Rd. IP14: S'ket 5B 6
St Peter's St. IP1: Ips 4B 36 (3D 4)
St Peter's Wlk. IP1: Ips 4D 4
St Raphael Ct. IP1: Ips 6G 27
St Stephen's Chu. La.
 IP1: Ips 3D 4
St Stephens La. IP1: Ips 3B 36 (2D 4)
Salehurst Rd. IP3: Ips 6B 38
Salisbury Rd. IP3: Ips 5F 37
Sallows Cl. IP1: Ips 2G 35
Sally Wood's La. IP6: C Mary 2F 11
Salmet Cl. IP2: Ips 6H 35
Salter Gdns. IP13: Grun 3F 21
Salthouse St. IP4: Ips 4C 36 (4F 5)
Samford Cl. IP9: Holb 1F 57
Samford Pl. IP8: Spro 3C 34
Samuel Ct. IP4: Ips 3C 36 (1F 5)
Sandhurst Av. IP3: Ips 5E 37
Sandling Cres. IP4: Rus A 4B 38
Sandlings, The IP3: Ips 2A 46
Sandown Cl. IP1: Ips 4H 27
Sandown Rd. IP1: Ips 4H 27
Sandpiper Rd. IP2: Ips 1F 43
Sandpit Cl. IP4: Rus A 4C 38
Sandringham Cl. IP2: Ips 1G 43
Sandy Cl. IP11: T Mart 1E 61
Sandyhill La. IP3: Ips 2D 44
Sandy La. CO11: Bran 4F 55
 IP6: Barh .2C 16
 IP6: C Mary 2E 11
 IP6: West .3C 28
 IP12: Mart, Wood 4D 32
 IP13: L Bea 3G 31
 IP13: W Mar 6G 13
Sapling Pl. IP4: Rus A 4B 38
Sawmill La. IP10: Nac 5E 47
Sawston Cl. IP2: Ips 1H 43
Sawyers Cl. IP9: Cap 2D 50
Saxon Cl. IP11: Fel 5E 63
Saxon Pk. IP6: N Mar 4B 10
Saxon Way IP12: Mel 4H 23
Schneider Cl. IP11: Fel 5C 64
School Cl. IP7: Had 4F 49
 IP9: Cap 2D 50
School Hill IP8: Wash 3A 42
School Ho's. IP13: Grun 2F 21
School La. CO7: Ded 6E 53
 CO7: E Ber 2G 53
 CO7: Stra M 3C 52
 CO11: Bran 4G 55
 IP12: Brom 3F 25
 IP12: Mart 4D 32
 IP13: Uff 5D 14
School Mdw. IP14: S'ket 2E 9
School Rd. IP6: Hen 1B 18
 IP9: S Gate 6H 59
 IP12: Wald 3H 41
School St. IP6: N Mar 4D 10
Schreiber Rd. IP4: Ips 2G 37

Scopes Rd. IP5: Kes 1F 39
Scott La. IP12: Mel 1B 24
Scott Rd. IP3: Ips 2G 45
Scrivener Dr. IP8: Ips 1C 42
Seabreeze Rd. IP14: S'ket 6C 6
Sea Rd. IP11: Fel 4D 64
Seaton Rd. IP11: Fel 6H 61
Seckford Almshouses IP12: Wood ...6G 23
Seckford Cl. IP4: Rus A 4C 38
Seckford Foundation IP12: Wood 6F 23
Seckford Hall Rd. IP13: Gt Bea, Wood . .2C 32
(not continuous)
Seckford St. IP12: Wood 6G 23
Seckford Ter. IP12: Wood 6G 23
Second Av. IP11: T Mary 4E 61
Sedan Wlk. IP1: Ips 4B 4
Selkirk Rd. IP4: Ips 1G 37
Selvale Way IP11: Fel 1D 64
Selwyn Cl. IP2: Ips 5B 36 (6C 4)
Semer Cl. IP14: S'ket 2E 9
Serpentine Rd. IP3: Ips 1G 45
Servite Ho. IP4: Ips 3E 37
Seven Cotts. IP5: Rus A 6H 29
Seven Cotts. La. IP5: Rus A 6H 29
Seven Gdns. Rd. IP13: Burg 2H 21
Severn Rd. IP3: Ips 6E 37
Sewell Wontner Cl. IP5: Kes 1F 39
Seymour Rd. IP2: Ips 5B 36 (6C 4)
Shackleton Rd. IP3: Ips 6G 37
Shackleton Sq. IP3: Ips 6G 37
Shaftesbury Sq. IP4: Ips 4C 36 (3F 5)
Shafto Rd. IP1: Ips 1F 35
Shakespeare Rd. IP1: Ips 3F 27
   IP14: S'ket 3B 6
Shamrock Av. IP2: Ips 5F 35
Shamrock Ho. IP1: Ips 5E 27
Shannon Rd. IP3: Ips 3F 45
Shaw Valley Rd. IP12: Mart 5C 32
Shearman Rd. IP7: Had 4G 49
Sheepdrift Rd. IP12: Brom 2H 25
Sheerwater Way IP14: S'ket 5G 7
Shelbourne Cl. IP5: Kes 2G 39
Sheldrake Dr. IP2: Ips 2E 43
Shelley Cl. IP14: S'ket 2F 9
Shelley St. IP2: Ips 5B 36 (6D 4)
Shenley Rd. IP3: Ips 2G 45
Shenstone Dr. IP8: Ips 4H 27
Shepherd Dr. IP8: Ips 1D 42
Shepherds La. IP9: Holb 3F 57
   IP14: S'ket 3A 6
Sheppards Way IP5: Kes 2G 39
Sherborne Av. IP4: Ips 5F 29
Sheridan Cl. IP14: S'ket 3A 6
Sheringham Ct. IP14: S'ket 6E 7
Sherrington Rd. IP1: Ips 1H 35
Sherwood Flds. IP5: Kes 2F 39
Shetland Cl. IP4: Ips 6F 29
Shimpling Cl. IP14: S'ket 2E 9
Ship La. IP8: Bram 6C 26
Ship Launch Rd. IP3: Ips 6C 36
Ship Mdw. Wlk. IP12: Wood 6H 23
Shire Hall 6H 23
Shire Hall Yd. IP4: Ips 4C 36 (4E 5)
Shirley Cl. IP1: Ips 4H 27
Shoebridge's Hill CO7: Ded 6D 52
Shortlands IP8: Ips 2E 43
SHOTLEY 3E 59
Shotley Cl. IP2: Ips 1D 42
   IP11: Fel 1C 64
SHOTLEY GATE 6H 59
Shotley Rd. IP9: Chel 3C 58
Shotley Wlk. IP9: S'ly 1E 59
Shrubbery Cl. IP11: Fel 1E 65
Shrubbery Rd. IP13: Has 4C 22
Shrubland Av. IP15: Mart H 6F 27
Shrubland Dr. IP4: Rus A 4C 38
Sidecentre Ga. IP5: Mart H 2B 40
(off Eagle Way)
Sidegate Av. IP4: Ips 1F 37
Sidegate La. IP4: Ips 6F 29
Sidegate La. W. IP4: Ips 6E 29
Silent St. IP1: Ips 4B 36 (3D 4)
Silk Mill Cl. IP7: Had 4E 49
Silverdale Av. IP14: S'ket 4C 6
Silverdale Cl. IP1: Ips 6H 27
Silver Leys IP9: B'ley 5H 51

Simon's Cross IP13: W Mar 4E 13
Simons Rd. IP12: Wood 4H 23
Simpson Cl. IP3: Ips 2E 45
Sinclair Dr. IP2: Ips 6B 36
Sir Alf Ramsey Way IP1: Ips 3A 4
Sirdar Rd. IP1: Ips 3H 35
Sir John Mills Theatre 2H 35
SKEET'S GREEN 1F 17
Skipper Rd. IP8: Ips 3F 43
Skylark La. IP8: Ips 1D 42
Slade, The IP6: Barh, Cla 3E 17
Slade St. IP4: Ips 4C 36 (4E 5)
Sleaford Cl. IP2: Ips 6H 35 (6A 4)
Slough Rd. CO7: E Ber 3F 55
   CO11: Bran 3F 55
Smart St. IP4: Ips 4C 36 (4E 5)
Smithers Cl. IP9: Cap 2D 50
Smithfield IP12: Mel 5A 24
Smiths Pl. IP5: Kes 2G 39
Snells La. IP11: Fel 4B 62
Snowcroft IP9: Cap 2D 50
Snowdon Hill IP13: W Mar 5F 13
Snowdon Rd. IP2: Ips 1A 44
Snow Hill Steps IP11: Fel 2E 65
(off Undercliff Rd. W.)
Snows Way CO11: Bran 5G 55
Soames Cl. IP14: S'ket 4C 6
Soane St. IP4: Ips 3C 36 (1E 5)
Solar Bowl 2E 35
Somerset Rd. IP4: Ips 1E 37
Somersham Rd. IP8: Bram 3A 26
Sorrel Cl. IP2: Ips 6G 35
Sorrel Horse M. IP4: Ips 4F 5
Sorrell Wlk. IP5: Mart H 2A 40
South Cl. IP4: Ips 1D 36
   IP12: Mel 1B 24
Southgate Rd. IP8: Ips 2C 42
South Hill IP11: Fel 2E 65
South St. IP1: Ips 2A 36 (1A 4)
South Vw. Grn. IP9: B'ley 5H 51
Spalding Cl. IP5: Kes 3E 39
Spanbies Rd. CO7: Stra M 4C 52
Speckled Wood Cl. IP8: Ips 3E 43
Speedwell Rd. IP2: Ips 5G 35
Spencer Way IP14: S'ket 4B 6
Spenser Rd. IP1: Ips 4F 27
Spike's La. IP14: S'ket 2B 6
Spindler Cl. IP5: Kes 2G 39
Spinney, The IP4: Rus A 5C 38
Spitfire Cl. IP3: Ips 2G 45
Spooners La. IP7: Had 3E 49
Springfield Av. IP11: Fel 6B 62
Springfield La. IP1: Ips 1G 35
Springhurst Cl. IP4: Ips 3E 37
Springland Cl. IP4: Ips 3F 37
Spring La. IP13: Uff 4E 15
   IP13: W Mar 4G 13
Spring Mdw. IP6: Play 3E 31
Spring Rd. IP4: Ips 3D 36 (2H 5)
Spring Row IP14: S'ket 4D 6
Springtail Rd. IP8: Ips 3F 43
Sprites End IP11: T Mary 4G 61
Spriteshall La. IP11: T Mary 4G 61
Sprites La. IP2: Ips 1D 42
   IP8: Ips 2D 42
SPROUGHTON 3C 34
Sproughton Bus. Pk. IP1: Ips 1D 34
Sproughton Ct. IP8: Spro 3B 34
Sproughton Rd. IP8: Ips, Spro 2C 34
Spur End IP12: Mel 4B 24
Square, The IP5: Mart H 2B 40
   IP7: Had 2F 49
   IP14: S'ket 1E 9
Squires La. IP5: Mart H 1B 40
Squirrels, The IP9: Cap 1D 50
Stable Ct. IP5: Mart H 5H 43
Stamford Cl. IP2: Ips 3G 43
Stammers Pl. IP5: Kes 1H 39
Stanley Av. IP3: Ips 5F 37
Stanley Rd. IP11: Fel 6H 61
Starfield Cl. IP4: Ips 3G 37
Starhouse La. IP14: One 5A 6
Star La. IP4: Ips 4B 36 (4D 4)
Station App. IP11: Fel 6B 62

Station Rd. IP6: Cla 5C 16
   IP7: Had 4E 49
   IP9: B'ley 5H 51
   IP11: T Mary 4F 61
   IP12: Mel 3B 24
   IP12: Wood 1H 33
Station Rd. E. IP14: S'ket 5E 7
Station Rd. W. IP14: S'ket 5D 6
Station St. IP2: Ips 6B 36 (6D 4)
Station Yd. IP2: Ips 5A 36 (5A 4)
   IP6: N Mar 4E 11
   IP7: Had 4F 49
Steggall Cl. IP6: N Mar 2C 10
Stella Maris IP2: Ips 4E 35
Stennetts Cl. IP11: T Mary 3E 61
Stephen Rd. IP5: Kes 1H 39
Stephen's Ct. IP4: Ips 3G 37
Stevenson Rd. IP1: Ips 3A 36 (2A 4)
Stewart Young Gro. IP5: Kes 2G 39
Stockmers End IP9: Cap 2D 50
Stockton Cl. IP7: Had 5G 49
STOKE 6D 4
Stokebridge Maltings IP2: Ips .5B 36 (5D 4)
Stoke Hall Rd. IP2: Ips 5B 36 (5C 4)
STOKE PARK 2H 43
Stoke Pk. Dr. IP2: Ips 3G 43
Stoke Pk. Gdns. IP2: Ips 2H 43
Stoke Quay IP2: Ips 5E 5
Stoke St. IP2: Ips 5B 36 (5C 4)
Stollery Cl. IP5: Kes 2F 39
Stonechat Rd. IP2: Ips 1D 42
Stonegrove Rd. IP11: Fel 4C 64
Stonehouse Rd. IP7: Had 3F 49
Stonelands Rd. IP11: Fel 5G 61
(off Runnacles Way)
Stone Lodge La. IP2: Ips 6H 35
Stone Lodge La. W. IP2: Ips 6G 35
Stone Lodge Wlk. IP2: Ips 6H 35
Stone Pl. IP12: Wood 6H 23
Stone St. IP7: Had 1B 48
Stoney Rd. IP13: Grun 1D 20
Stopford Ct. IP1: Ips 2H 35
Stour Av. IP11: Fel 2D 64
Stourside IP9: S Gate 6G 59
Stour Valley Path CO7: E Ber 6A 54
Stour Vw. CO7: Ded 6E 53
Stowe Lodge IP14: One 4A 6
STOWMARKET 5D 6
Stowmarket Rd.
   IP6: Bad, N Mar ....3H 9 & 1A 10
   IP6: Gt Bla 1A 16
   IP14: O New 2D 6
   IP14: S'and 4F 7
Stowmarket Station (Rail) 5E 7
STOWUPLAND 2H 7
Stowupland Rd. IP14: S'ket 4E 7
Stowupland St. IP14: S'ket 5E 7
Stradbroke Rd. IP4: Ips 2F 37
Straight Rd. IP10: Fox 3F 47
Strand, The IP2: Wher 3B 44
Stratford Ct. IP1: Ips 4G 27
Stratford Rd. CO7: Ded 6B 52
   IP1: Ips 5F 27
STRATFORD ST MARY 4C 52
STRATFORD ST MARY INTERCHANGE 3D 52
Strawberry Hill IP6: Wit 3D 18
Street, The CO7: E Ber 3G 53
   CO7: Stra M 4B 52
   IP6: Tudd 2H 29
   IP6: Wit 4F 19
   IP8: Bel 5D 42
   IP8: Bram 4A 26
   IP8: Wash 3A 42
   IP9: Cap 2C 50
   IP9: Holb 1E 57
   IP9: S'ly 3E 59
   IP9: Wher 5H 43
   IP10: Nac 6E 47
   IP12: Eyk 1H 25
   IP12: Mel 4D 32
   IP12: Mel 4B 24
   IP12: New 6H 41
   IP13: Grun 3F 21
   IP13: L Bea 3G 31
   IP13: Leth 1A 12
   IP13: Pett 1E 15

Street Farm Cl. IP10: Buc 6H 47
Stricklands Rd. IP14: S'ket 6E 7
Strickmere CO7: Stra M 4B 52
Struggler's La. IP6: Wit 5F 19
Stuart Cl. IP4: Ips 2E 37
  IP11: Fel 4E 63
Stubbins La. CO7: Stra M 1F 53
Stubbs Cl. IP3: Ips 2F 45
Stump St. IP13: Pett 2D 14
Sturdee Av. IP3: Ips 6G 37
STUTTON 6B 56
Stutton Cl. IP9: Sutt 6C 56
Stutton La. IP9: Tatt 4A 56
Sub-Station Rd. IP11: Fel 3C 64
Sudbourne Rd. IP11: Fel 6G 61
Sudbury Rd. IP11: Fel 1B 64
Suffolk Ent. Cen. IP1: Ips 4A 4
Suffolk Pl. IP12: Wood 6A 24
Suffolk Retail Pk. IP1: Ips 3H 35
Suffolk Rd. IP4: Ips 2C 36 (1F 5)
Suffolk Sands Holiday Pk.
  IP11: Fel 5C 64
Suffolk Showground 2D 46
Suffolk Water Pk. 2B 26
Sullivan Pl. IP12: Wald 3H 41
Summerfield Cl. IP4: Ips 1A 38
Summerfield Ct. IP4: Ips 1A 38
Summer La. IP12: Brom 3F 25
Sunderland Rd. IP11: Fel 5C 64
Sunfield Cl. IP4: Ips 3G 37
Sun La. IP12: Wood 6H 23
Sunningdale Av. IP4: Ips 4A 38
Sunningdale Dr. IP11: Fel 5C 62
Sunray Av. IP11: Fel 5C 62
Surbiton Rd. IP1: Ips 1G 35
Surrey Rd. IP1: Ips 3H 35
  IP11: Fel 1E 65
Sutton Cl. IP12: Wood 6A 24
Sutton Grn. IP9: Sutt 6E 57
Sutton Hoo Vis. Cen. 6D 24
Sutton Rd. IP12: Brom, Sutt 5D 24
Swallow Cl. IP11: Fel 4D 62
Swallow Dr. IP14: S'ket 6G 7
Swallow Rd. IP2: Ips 6D 34
Swallowtail Cl. IP8: Ips 3F 43
Swan Cl. IP5: Mart H 2C 40
  IP14: S'ket .5B 6
Swan Hill IP8: Wash 2A 42
Swan La. IP6: West 3D 28
Swan Mdw. CO7: Stra M 4B 52
Swansea Av. IP2: Ips 2A 44
Swatchway Cl. IP3: Ips 4G 45
Swaynes CO7: Stra M 3B 52
Swift Dr. IP14: S'ket 5G 7
Swinburne Rd. IP1: Ips 4F 27
Swinton Cl. IP2: Ips 2E 43
Sycamore Cl. IP8: Ips 2D 42
Sycamore Rd. IP14: S'and 3G 7
Sycamore Way CO11: Bran 4G 55
Sydney Brown Ct. IP7: Had 4E 49
  (off Magdalen Rd.)

T

Tacket St. IP4: Ips 4C 36 (3E 5)
Tacon Rd. IP11: Fel 4D 64
Takers La. IP14: S'ket 1E 9
Tallboys Cl. IP5: Kes 1F 39
Tally Ho Cnr. CO7: Stra M 4C 52
Talmash Gdns. IP2: Ips 5H 35
Tanners Vw. IP1: Ips 2G 35
Tannery Rd. IP14: Comb 5C 8
Tanyard Cl. IP12: Wood 1H 33
Tarn Hows Cl. IP11: Fel 5E 63
Tasmania Rd. IP4: Ips 3A 38
TATTINGSTONE 1A 56
Taunton Cl. IP1: Ips 3A 28
Taunton Rd. IP11: Fel 5A 62
Tavern St. IP1: Ips 3B 36 (2D 4)
  IP14: S'ket .5D 6
Tawney Cl. IP9: Cap 2D 50
Tayler Cl. IP7: Had 4E 49
Tayler Rd. IP7: Had 4E 49
Teal Cl. IP2: Ips 6E 35
Temple Pattle CO11: Bran 6F 55

Temple Rd. IP3: Ips 5H 37
  IP14: S'ket .6D 6
Tenby Rd. IP2: Ips 2A 44
Tennyson Cl. IP12: Wood 5F 23
Tennyson Rd. IP4: Ips 4E 37
Tenter Fld. CO7: Stra M 4C 52
Tern Rd. IP2: Ips 1F 43
Terry Gdns. IP5: Kes 2H 39
Thackeray Gro. IP14: S'ket 4B 6
Thackeray Rd. IP1: Ips 4F 27
Thanet Rd. IP4: Ips 3G 37
Thatchers Wlk. IP14: S'ket 2D 8
Theatre St. IP12: Wood 6G 23
Theberton Rd. IP3: Ips 2G 45
Theobald Cl. IP6: N Mar 3D 10
Thetford Rd. IP1: Ips 2H 35
Thirling Ct. IP5: Mart H 3B 40
Thirlmere Cl. IP11: Fel 5E 63
Thirlmere Dr. IP14: S'ket 5B 6
Thistle Cl. IP2: Ips 5G 35
Thomasarne Cl. IP14: S'ket 3C 6
Thomas Av. IP11: T Mary 3F 61
Thomas Chyd. Cl. IP12: Mel 6C 14
Thomas Walls Cl. IP13: Grun 3G 21
Thomas Young Cl. IP14: S'ket 2D 8
Thompson Cl. IP13: Grun 3F 21
Thompson Rd. IP1: Ips 1G 35
Thong Hall Rd. IP13: Pett, W Mar 5D 12
Thornbush La. IP8: Bram 1A 34
THORNEY GREEN 3G 7
Thorney Grn. Rd. IP14: S'and 3G 7
Thorney Rd. IP9: Cap 2C 50
Thornhayes Cl. IP2: Ips 6H 35
Thornhill Rd. IP6: Barh, Cla 3D 16
Thornley Dr. IP4: Ips 1H 37
Thornley Rd. IP11: Fel 1H 65
Thorn Way IP11: Fel 1D 64
Thoroughfare IP1: Ips 2D 4
  IP12: Wood 6H 23
THORPE COMMON 1B 60
Thorpe La. IP11: T Mart 1B 60
Threadneedle St. CO7: Ded 6D 52
  IP7: Had 3E 49
Three Stiles La. IP12: Mart 5D 32
Through Duncans IP12: Wood 1F 33
Through Jollys IP5: Kes 1G 39
Thurleston La. IP1: Ips 2G 27
Thurlow Ct. IP14: S'ket 5D 6
Thurmans La. IP11: T Mart 2F 61
  IP11: T Mary 3E 61
Thurston Ct. IP11: Fel 2B 64
Tide Mill 1H 33
Tide Mill Way IP12: Wood 1H 33
Timperley Cl. IP7: Had 2E 49
Timperley Rd. IP7: Had 2F 49
Tinabrook Cl. IP2: Ips 2F 43
Tintern Cl. IP2: Ips 1H 43
Tippet Av. IP14: S'ket 3C 6
Titchwell Dr. IP3: Ips 3A 46
Tokio Rd. IP4: Ips 3F 37
Toller Rd. IP3: Ips 6D 36
Toll Ga. Rd. IP9: Cap 2D 50
Tolly Cobbold Brewery Tap & Mus.
  . . . . .6D 36
Tolworth Rd. IP4: Ips 3F 37
Tomline Ct. IP10: Nac 6E 47
Tomline Rd. IP3: Ips 4F 37
  IP11: Fel 2F 65
Tomo Ind. Est. IP14: S'ket 5F 7
Tooley's Ct. IP4: Ips 3E 5
Topplesfield Cl. IP7: Had 4E 49
Topplesfield Gdns.
  IP7: Had 4D 48
Top Rd. IP13: Has 3C 22
Top St. IP12: Mart 3D 32
Tortoiseshell Cl. IP8: Ips 3F 43
Touchey's La. CO7: E Ber 4C 54
Tourist Info. Cen.
  Dedham 6E 53
  Felixstowe .2E 65
  Flatford 6A 54
  Ipswich 3B 36 (2D 4)
  Stowmarket .5D 6
  Woodbridge 1H 33
Tovell's Rd. IP4: Ips 3E 37
Tovell St. IP13: Uff 5D 14

Tower Chu. Yd. IP1: Ips 2D 4
Tower Mill La. IP7: Had 3F 49
Tower Mill Rd. IP1: Ips 2G 35
Tower Ramparts IP1: Ips 3B 36 (1C 4)
  (not continuous)
Tower Ramparts Shop. Cen.
  IP1: Ips 3B 36 (2D 4)
Tower Rd. IP11: Fel 2E 65
Tower St. IP1: Ips 3B 36 (2D 4)
Town Grn. IP14: S'ket 5C 6
Town La. IP13: Grun 2G 21
Trafalgar Cl. IP4: Ips 3E 37
Tranmere Gro. IP1: Ips 5G 27
Treetops IP11: Fel 4H 61
Treeview IP14: S'ket 5B 6
Trefoil Cl. IP2: Ips 5G 35
Trelawny Ho. IP11: Fel 4C 64
Tremlett La. IP5: Kes 2A 40
Tremlett Rd. IP3: Ips 1E 45
Trevose IP11: Fel 1G 65
TRIMLEY LOWER STREET 3C 60
Trimley Marshes Nature Reserve 5A 60
Trimley Marshes Nature Reserve Vis. Cen.
  . . . . .6A 60
TRIMLEY ST MARTIN 1E 61
TRIMLEY ST MARY 4F 61
Trimley Station (Rail) 4F 61
Trinity Av. IP11: Fel 2A 64
Trinity Cl. IP5: Kes 2C 38
  IP12: Wood 2E 33
Trinity Ind. Est. IP11: Fel 3B 64
Trinity St. IP3: Ips 5D 36 (6H 5)
Trinity Wlk. IP14: S'and 2H 7
Troon Gdns. IP4: Ips 6G 29
Truro Cres. IP5: Kes 3D 38
Tuddenham Av. IP4: Ips 2D 36 (1G 5)
Tuddenham La. IP5: Rus A, Tudd 5G 29
  IP6: Wit 4G 19
TUDDENHAM ST MARTIN 2H 29
Tudor Cl. IP9: S Gate 5G 59
Tudor Pl. IP4: Ips 3C 36 (2F 5)
Turban, The IP12: Wood 6H 23
Turino Av. IP5: Mart H 2D 40
Turin St. IP2: Ips 5B 36 (6D 4)
Turnbull Cl. IP5: Kes 2H 39
Turner Gdns. IP12: Wood 2E 33
Turner Gro. IP5: Kes 1G 39
Turner Rd. IP3: Ips 3F 45
  IP14: S'ket .4B 6
Turn La. IP12: Wood 1H 33
Turnpike La. IP12: Mel 5A 24
Turret Grn. Ct. IP1: Ips 4B 36 (3D 4)
Turret La. IP1: Ips 4B 36 (3D 4)
Twelve Acre App. IP5: Kes 2E 39
Twinnings, The IP14: S'ket 2C 8
Two Acres IP9: Cap 1E 51
Two Ho. Cl. IP13: W Mar 4F 13
Tydemans Cl. IP14: S'ket 5D 6
Tye La. IP8: Bram 4A 26
Tylers Grn. IP11: T Mary 4F 61
Tyler St. IP2: Ips 5C 36 (6E 5)
Tylers Way IP14: S'ket 2D 8
Tymmes Pl. IP13: Has 3D 22
Tyndale Gdns. IP11: Fel 6D 62
Tyrone Cl. IP1: Ips 5E 27

U

UCG Cinema 4C 4
UFFORD 6E 15
Ufford Pl. IP13: Uff 6E 15
Ufford Rd. IP12: Brom, Eyk 1F 25
  IP13: Bred .5A 14
Ullswater Av. IP11: Fel 4E 63
Ulster Av. IP1: Ips 6E 27
Undercliff IP11: Fel 2F 65
Undercliff Rd. E. IP11: Fel 1H 65
Undercliff Rd. W. IP11: Fel 1G 65
Underhill IP14: S'ket 6C 6
Union Rd. IP14: One 4A 6
Union St. IP2: Ips 3C 36 (2E 5)
Union St. E. IP14: S'ket 5D 6
Union St. W. IP14: S'ket 5D 6
  (not continuous)

Unity Rd. IP14: S'ket 6D 6
Unity St. IP3: Ips 5D 36 (5H 5)
University Suffolk College 3G 5
Upland Rd. IP4: Ips 3F 37
Up. Barclay St. IP4: Ips 4C 36 (2E 5)
Up. Brook St. IP4: Ips 3B 36 (3D 4)
Up. Cavendish St.
    IP3: Ips .4F 37
Up. High St. IP1: Ips 2B 36 (1C 4)
Up. Melton Ter. IP12: Mel 1C 24
Up. Moorfield Rd. IP12: Wood 5G 23
Up. Orwell Cotts. IP4: Ips 3E 5
Up. Orwell St. IP4: Ips 4C 36 (3E 5)
UPPER STREET
    Colchester 1A 52
    Ipswich .6A 56
Upper St. CO7: Stra M 4B 52
    IP6: Wit .1F 19
Upsons Way IP5: Kes 1H 39
Upton Cl. IP4: Ips 3D 36 (2H 5)
Uvedale Ct. IP6: N Mar 4E 11
Uvedale Gdns. IP6: N Mar 4E 11
Uxbridge Cres. IP3: Ips 2H 45

V

Vale La. IP7: Ker 1A 48
Valiant Rd. IP5: Mart H 2B 40
Valley Cl. CO11: Bran 4G 55
    IP1: Ips .6B 28
    IP12: Wood 6H 23
Valley Farm Carmargue Horses
    . . . . .3H 23
Valley Farm Dr. IP8: Spro 6A 34
Valley Farm La. IP7: Had 4H 49
    IP12: Mel 3H 23
Valley Farm Rd. IP12: Mel 3H 23
Valley Rd. IP1: Ips 2H 35
    IP4: Ips .2H 35
Valleyview Dr.
    IP4: Rus A 5C 38
Valley Vw. Ri. IP12: Mart 4D 32
Valley Wlk. IP11: Fel 6A 62
Vandyck Cl. IP3: Ips 3F 45
Vaughan St. IP2: Ips 5B 36 (6D 4)
Ventris Cl. IP2: Ips 4E 35
Vere Gdns. IP1: Ips 5B 28
Vermont Cres. IP4: Ips 2C 36
Vermont Rd. IP4: Ips 2C 36
Verneuil Av. IP14: S'ket 2C 8
Vernon St. IP2: Ips 5B 36 (5D 4)
Veyses End CO7: Stra M 3C 52
Vicarage Cl. IP8: Bram 6C 26
Vicarage Hill IP12: Wood 6H 23
Vicarage La. IP8: Bram 6C 26
    IP9: Wher 6A 44
Vicarage Rd. IP11: Fel 1C 64
Victoria Rd. IP11: Fel 2E 65
    IP12: Wood 6H 23
    IP14: S'ket 4E 7
Victoria St. IP1: Ips 3H 35
    IP11: Fel .1F 65
Victory Rd. IP4: Ips 2F 37
View Point Rd. IP11: Fel 6B 64
Vigar Av. IP5: Kes 1F 39
Viking Cl. IP12: Mart 5D 32
Viking Hgts. IP12: Mart 5D 32
Viking Rd. IP14: S'ket 6C 6
Vincent Cl. IP1: Ips 1F 35
Vincent Drift IP5: Kes 2A 40
Vinery Cl. IP13: W Mar 5F 13
Vine Wlk. IP9: Cap 2D 50
Vinnicombe Ct. IP2: Ips 2F 43
Violet Cl. IP2: Ips 5G 35
Violet Hill Rd. IP14: S'ket 4C 6
Visdelou Ter. IP9: S Gate 5H 59

W

Wadgate Rd. IP11: Fel 1D 64
Wadhurst Rd. IP3: Ips 6A 38
Wainwright Gdns. IP6: Gt Bla 3A 16
Wainwright Way IP5: Kes 1G 39
WALDRINGFIELD 3H 41

WALDRINGFIELD HEATH 3F 41
Waldringfield Rd. IP10: Brig 4C 40
    IP12: Mart 5E 33
Walk, The IP1: Ips 3B 36 (2D 4)
    IP5: Kes .1E 39
    IP11: Fel .5H 61
                                     (not continuous)
Walker Chase IP5: Kes 3F 39
Walker Cl. IP3: Ips 4H 37
Wallace Rd. IP1: Ips 1F 35
Wallers Gro. IP2: Ips 5G 35
Walnut Cl. IP11: Fel 4E 63
Walnuts, The IP13: Uff 5D 14
Walnuts La. IP13: Pett, W Mar 6E 13
Walnut Tree Cl. IP8: Bram 5B 26
Walnut Tree Wlk. IP14: S'ket 5C 6
Walsingham Ct. IP2: Ips 3G 43
Waltham Cl. IP2: Ips 1H 43
WALTON 5A 62
Walton Av. IP11: Fel 3C 64
Walton Cl. IP14: S'ket 3B 6
Walton Ho. IP1: Ips 2A 4
Walton Rd. IP11: Fel 2A 64
Ward Cl. IP7: Had 1E 49
Wardley Cl. IP2: Ips 2E 43
Ward Rd. IP8: Ips 2C 42
Wareham Av. IP3: Ips 6A 38
Warren Chase IP5: Kes 2H 39
WARREN HEATH 2C 46
Warren Heath Av. IP3: Ips 1A 46
Warren Heath Rd. IP3: Ips 1A 46
Warren Hill Rd. IP12: Wood 1F 33
Warren La. IP5: Mart H 2B 40
    IP9: Chel, Erw 5D 58
Warrington Rd. IP1: Ips 2A 36
Warwick Av. IP12: Wood 5G 23
Warwick Rd. IP4: Ips 3D 36 (1H 5)
WASHBROOK 2A 42
WASHBROOK STREET 6A 34
Wash La. IP6: Wit 2F 19
    IP14: Gt Fin, One 5A 6
Waterford Rd. IP1: Ips 5E 27
Waterhead La. IP12: Mel 3C 24
Water La. IP7: Ker 1A 48
    IP13: W Mar 5H 13
Waterloo Rd. IP1: Ips 1F 35
Waterworks St. IP4: Ips 4C 36 (3F 5)
Watery La. IP13: Has 3B 22
Watts Cl. IP4: Ips 4C 36 (3E 5)
Waveney Rd. IP1: Ips 1F 35
Wayside Cl. IP14: S'ket 2D 8
Weaver Cl. IP1: Ips 1E 35
Weavers Cl. IP7: Had 3E 49
    IP14: S'ket 2C 8
Weavers Way IP6: Barh 4C 16
Webb Rd. IP14: S'ket 2D 8
Webb's Cl. IP1: Comb 4C 8
Webbs Ct. IP5: Kes 2F 39
Webb St. IP2: Ips 6B 36 (6D 4)
Welbeck Cl. IP11: T Mary 4G 61
Welhams Way CO11: Bran 5G 55
Wellesley Rd. IP4: Ips 4E 37
Well Fld. IP6: Hen 2A 18
Wellington Cl. IP7: Had 2E 49
Wellington Ct. IP1: Ips 5D 62
                                (off Wellington St.)
Wellington St. IP1: Ips 2H 35
Wells Cl. IP1: Ips 3D 36 (2F 5)
Wendy Cl. IP9: Chel 3C 58
Wenham La. CO7: Gt Wen 4A 50
Wentworth Cl. IP7: Had 4G 49
Wentworth Dr. IP8: Ips 1D 42
    IP11: Fel .5D 62
Wesel Av. IP11: Fel 1C 64
Wesley Way IP1: Ips 1G 35
WESTBOURNE 1G 35
Westbourne Rd. IP1: Ips 6G 27
Westbury Rd. IP4: Ips 5E 37
West End Rd. IP1: Ips 4H 35 (4A 4)
WESTERFIELD 3D 28
Westerfield Bus. Cen. IP6: West 4D 28
Westerfield Ct. IP4: Ips 2C 36
Westerfield La. IP6: Tudd 3F 29
Westerfield Rd. IP4: Ips 2C 36
    IP6: West .3D 28

Westerfield Station (Rail) 4D 28
Western Av. IP11: Fel 5E 63
Western Cl. IP4: Rus A 5C 38
Western's End CO11: Bran 5G 55
Westgate St. IP1: Ips 3B 36 (2C 4)
Westholme Cl. IP12: Wood 1G 33
Westholme Rd. IP1: Ips 6H 27
Westland IP5: Mart H 2B 40
West Lawn IP4: Ips 1G 37
Westleton Way IP11: Fel 6G 61
West Lodge IP6: N Mar 2D 10
West Mdws. IP1: Ips 3D 26
West Mill Grn. IP9: B'ley 5G 51
Westminster Cl. IP4: Ips 4G 37
Westmorland Rd. IP11: Fel 4E 63
Weston Ct. IP14: S'ket 6D 6
West Rd. IP3: Ips 3B 46
West Vw. CO7: Ded 6F 53
    IP14: S'ket 5B 6
Westwood Av. IP1: Ips 1H 35
Westwood Cl. IP1: Ips 2H 35
Wetherby Cl. IP1: Ips 3A 28
Wexford Rd. IP1: Ips 5E 27
Weyland Rd. IP6: Wit 1F 19
Weymouth Rd. IP4: Ips 3E 37
Wharfedale Rd. IP1: Ips 6H 27
Whatfield Way IP14: S'ket 2E 9
Wheelwrights, The IP11: T Mary 3F 61
Wherry La. IP4: Ips 4F 5
WHERSTEAD 5A 44
Wherstead Rd. IP2: Ips 3B 44
Whinchat Cl. IP2: Ips 6E 35
Whincroft IP13: W Mar 6F 13
Whinfield IP5: Mart H 1A 40
Whinfield Ct. IP5: Mart H 1B 40
Whinneys, The IP5: Kes 1G 39
Whinyard Way IP11: Fel 4E 63
Whitby Rd. IP4: Ips 1E 37
White Elm St. IP3: Ips 5D 36 (5H 5)
White Foot La. IP13: Burg 1G 21
White Horse Cl. IP11: Fel 5D 62
White Horse Rd. CO7: E Ber 4A 54
    IP9: Cap .2E 51
WHITE HOUSE 4D 26
Whitehouse Ind. Est. IP1: Ips 4D 26
White Ho. Rd. IP1: Ips 4D 26
White Lion Ct. IP7: Had 4E 49
                                      (off High St.)
White Lodge Gdns. IP5: Kes 1F 39
Whites Fld. CO7: E Ber 2G 53
Whitethorn Rd. IP3: Pur F 2C 46
Whitland Cl. IP2: Ips 3H 43
Whittle Rd. IP2: Ips 3G 35
WHITTON 4G 27
Whitton Chu. La. IP1: Ips 3F 27
Whitton La. IP1: Ips 3E 27
Whitton Leyer IP8: Bram 5D 26
Whitworth Cl. IP1: Ips 1E 43
Wickhambrook Ct. IP11: Fel 1B 64
WICKHAM MARKET 5F 13
Wickham Mkt. IP13: East, Hach 1C 12
Wicklow Rd. IP1: Ips 5E 27
Widgeon Cl. IP2: Ips 6G 35
Wigmore Cl. IP2: Ips 2G 43
Wilberforce St. IP1: Ips 2H 35 (1A 4)
Wilderness La. IP12: Wood 5H 23
Wilding Ct. IP12: Wood 1F 33
Wilding Dr. IP5: Kes 2G 39
Wilding Rd. IP8: Ips 2C 42
Wilford Bri. Rd. IP12: Mel 4B 24
Wilford Bri. Spur IP12: Mel 4B 24
Wilfred Hurry Cl. IP8: Bram 6B 26
Wilkes Ct. IP5: Kes 2H 39
Wilkes Way IP14: S'ket 5D 6
Wilkinson Dr. IP5: Kes 3F 39
Wilkinson Way IP12: Mel 5H 23
Willets Pond CO7: E Ber 4A 54
William Booth Way IP11: Fel 6G 61
William Ho. IP4: Ips 3C 36 (1F 5)
William Paul Tenements IP2: Ips 6C 4
Williamsport Way IP6: N Mar 5F 11
William St. IP1: Ips 3B 36 (1D 4)
Willoughby Rd. IP2: Ips 5A 36 (5B 4)
Willow Cl. IP6: Cla 5D 16
Willowcroft Rd. IP1: Ips 5H 27

Willows, The. IP5: Rus A 6B **30**
Willow Tree Cl. IP13: W Mar 5E **13**
Willow Wlk. IP6: N Mar 2D **10**
Wilmslow Av. IP12: Wood 6F **23**
Wilmslow Dr. IP2: Ips 1D **42**
Wilson Rd. IP7: Had 4F **49**
  IP8: Ips 2C **42**
Wimborne Av. IP3: Ips 5A **38**
Wimpole Cl. IP5: Rus A 3C **38**
Wincanton Cl. IP4: Ips 6F **29**
Winchester Cl. IP14: S'ket 5B **6**
Winchester Gdns. IP6: Barh 3E **17**
Winchester Way IP2: Ips 3G **43**
Windermere Cl. IP3: Ips 3G **45**
Windermere Rd. IP11: Fel 4E **63**
  IP14: S'ket 5C **6**
Windiate Ct. *IP5: Kes* *2G* ***39***
                (off Ropes Dr.)
Winding Piece Wlk. IP9: Cap 2D **50**
Windmill Hill IP9: Cap 2B **50**
Windrush Rd. IP5: Kes 1F **39**
Windsor Rd. IP1: Ips 2G **35**
  IP11: Fel 2D **64**
Winfrith Rd. IP3: Ips 5A **38**
Wingate Ho. *IP1: Ips* *2H* ***35***
             (off Bramford Rd.)
Wingfield St. IP4: Ips 4C **36** (3E **5**)
Winifred Fison Ho's. IP12: Mel 3B **24**
Winston Av. IP4: Ips 1H **37**
Winston Cl. IP11: Fel 6G **61**
Withipoll St. IP4: Ips 3C **36** (1E **5**)
WITNESHAM 3F **19**
Witnesham Chu. La. IP6: Wit 3F **19**
Witnesham Rd. IP6: West, Wit 1E **29**
Wolsey Gdns. IP11: Fel 2F **65**
Wolsey Rd. IP14: S'ket 4C **6**
Wolsey St. IP1: Ips 4B **36** (4C **4**)
Wolsey Theatre 2B **4**
Wolton Rd. IP5: Kes 2F **39**
Wolves Farm La. IP7: Had 1H **49**
WOODBRIDGE 6H **23**
Woodbridge Mus. 6H **23**

Woodbridge Rd. IP4: Ips 3C **36** (2E **5**)
  IP4: Rus A 2A **38**
  IP5: Rus A 2A **38**
  IP12: New 5H **41**
  IP13: Grun, Has 2G **21**
Woodbridge Rd. E. IP4: Ips 2H **37**
Woodbridge Station (Rail) 1H **33**
Woodcock Rd. IP2: Ips 1F **43**
Woodcote IP14: S'ket 5B **6**
Wood Cotts. IP5: Rus A 6H **29**
Wood Farm Rd. IP13: Grun 4C **20**
Woodfield Dr. IP14: S'ket 6E **7**
Woodfield La. IP9: Sutt 5A **56**
  IP14: S'ket 6D **6**
Woodgates Rd. CO7: E Ber 5A **50**
Woodhouse La. IP10: Fox 1F **47**
Woodhouse Sq. IP4: Ips 4C **36** (3F **5**)
Woodlands IP2: Ips 2D **42**
  IP7: Had 2C **48**
  IP9: Chel 3B **58**
Woodlands Rd. IP9: Holb 1E **57**
Woodlands Way IP1: Ips 3D **26**
Woodlark Cl. IP2: Ips 2F **43**
Woodpecker Cl. IP14: S'ket 6G **7**
Woodpecker Rd. IP2: Ips 6E **35**
Woodrush Rd. IP3: Pur F 1A **46**
Woodside IP5: Mart H 1D **40**
  IP14: S'ket 5B **6**
Woods La. IP12: Mel, Wood 4G **23**
Wood Spring Cl. IP2: Ips 1H **43**
Woodstone Av. IP1: Ips 6B **28**
Woodthorpe Cl. IP7: Had 4G **49**
Woodthorpe Rd. IP7: Had 4F **49**
Woodville Rd. IP4: Ips 4E **37** (3H **5**)
Woodward Cl. IP2: Ips 4E **35**
Woollards Cl. IP1: Ips 3H **35**
Woolmers Cl. IP14: S'ket 1D **8**
Woolner Cl. IP6: Barh 4C **16**
  IP7: Had 3F **49**
Woolnough Rd. IP12: Wood 5G **23**

Woolnoughs, The IP5: Kes 2G **39**
Woolverstone Cl. IP2: Ips 2D **42**
Worcester Rd. IP3: Ips 3F **45**
Wordsworth Cres. IP1: Ips 4F **27**
Wordsworth Rd. IP14: S'ket 3B **6**
Workshop La. IP10: Nac 6F **47**
Worsley Cl. IP2: Ips 1E **43**
Wren Av. IP2: Ips 6E **35**
Wren Cl. IP14: S'ket 5G **7**
Wrens Pk. IP11: Fel 4E **63**
Wright Cl. IP14: S'ket 2D **8**
Wright La. IP5: Kes 1G **39**
Wright Rd. IP3: Ips 1H **45**
Wroxham Rd. IP3: Ips 6E **37**
Wye Rd. IP3: Ips 6F **37**
Wykes Bishop St. IP3: Ips 5D **36** (5G **5**)
Wynterton Cl. IP3: Ips 2G **45**
Wynton Ri. IP14: S'ket 1E **9**
Wyseman Pl. CO11: Catt 6F **55**
Wyvern Rd. IP3: Ips 2H **45**

Y

Yarmouth Rd. IP1: Ips 3H **35**
  IP12: Mel 3B **24**
  IP13: Mel, Uff 3B **24**
  IP13: Uff 4D **14**
Yeoman Cres. IP7: Had 4F **49**
Yeoman Rd. IP11: Fel 2C **64**
Yeoman Way IP7: Had 4F **49**
Yetton Ward Ho. IP11: Fel 6H **61**
Yew Ct. IP2: Ips 6H **35**
Yewtree Gro. IP5: Kes 2C **38**
Yew Tree Ri. IP13: W Mar 4F **13**
Yewtree Ri. IP8: Ips 2D **42**
York Cres. IP6: Cla 4D **16**
York Rd. IP3: Ips 5F **37**
  IP5: Mart H 3B **40**
  IP11: Fel 1F **65**